GLOVES OFF

40 Years of Unfiltered Sports Writing

LOWELL COHN

Forewords by Steve Young *&* Brian Murphy

Afterword by Jim Harbaugh

 Roundtree Press
Petaluma, California

For Robert Cohn, my brother
1941–2018

CONTENTS

FOREWORD
BY STEVE YOUNG

LOWELL COHN WAS TOUGH, absolutely brutal sometimes. He was like the power-washer blasting the barnacles off the boat—a steel-wool scouring pad extricating any and all blemishes from the pan, no matter how ingrained they might be.

Simply put, you did not want to be the subject of one of Lowell's columns, but you always read them. In some ways, I felt like Lowell never worried about his next column. "If I were worried about my next column, I wouldn't write this!" He didn't do fluff. He was as unvarnished and unapologetic as we've ever seen in the Bay Area, and the fans benefited from that raw, unclouded approach. And we did, too.

As tough as he was, I am thankful for Lowell Cohn. He made me better; he made the team and our entire organization better. I'm not sure all my teammates would agree, but his voice was necessary to keep us on track. It was medicine that was good for you. It didn't taste good, but it was good for you in the end.

It took me awhile to understand where Lowell was coming from, but once I did, I realized we were interested in the same things. Football is a human lab, and if you want to change behavior, you have to figure out what drives behavior. That's what Lowell was pursuing and so was I.

He wasn't interested in the Xs and Os as much as he was interested in the human drama that surrounded him. He wanted to deconstruct why you were losing, but he didn't want to hear "dropped passes or missed throws." He wanted to get underneath it. He didn't want to just hang around the edges of a conversation or a subject. He wanted to get to the soft, unexposed places to try to get to why it was happening. It made him unique and a must-read.

For a half decade, Joe Montana and I found ourselves right in the middle of Lowell's coverage, which was very uncomfortable. The quarterback controversy provided the human drama that Lowell relished. He was absolutely relentless as he tried to crack the case.

It taught me early on that when you're in a tough job, Lowell made it tougher. When you're dealing with all the challenging issues day to day, the last thing you needed was something that wasn't going to help you ease through it. Lowell was never going to help you ease through it. He would make sure you got every inch of it.

But in the end, we were better because of Lowell. There's always a need for a voice like that. It's important. Nothing is worse than internal marketing; it is death to great organizations. It's when we're telling each other that we're all great and everything is fine. That didn't happen with Lowell. As a truth-seeker, he wouldn't allow it. His nonmarketing voice was ever-present and ensured that we were never just an echo chamber. It absolutely made a difference.

And the truth is, I loved to try to prove him wrong when he was tough. If he had an opinion about your abilities because that's what he was digging at—what you can't do—I was going to show him he was wrong.

I remember Bill Walsh told him one day, "I don't know where this kid, Steve, is. No one knows where he is." And Lowell took that as a theme— "he's just crazy and runs around." Well, that's not true. I am someone who's focused on doing the job. I don't want to just run around and be crazy. I knew he was wrong and I set out to prove it.

And as tough as he could be, I always enjoyed the interaction. Lowell is a philosopher. He has a unique take on the human condition and it led to many wholesome discussions between us that I always appreciated. I can honestly say that we have never had an uninteresting conversation.

His impact on Bay Area sports is significant. He was the kind of guy who could change the trajectory of a situation, of a season, of a career. What Lowell said mattered, whether you liked it or not. It was always a lot easier when he was writing about someone else, but you always paid attention.

FOREWORD
BY BRIAN MURPHY

The great news is, my friend Lowell Cohn wrote a book.

The bad news is, all it does is make me want more writing from Lowell.

Reading Lowell again makes me want to drive over to his house, maybe with that Cakebread Chardonnay he brought to Bill Walsh's house, open the bottle, and negotiate again how we can get Lowell Cohn's writing back into our lives on a daily basis.

Lowell retired a couple of years ago, after one of the most impactful sports-writing careers in Bay Area history. Lowell was different from all of us. He was better. He didn't do California passive-aggressive. I don't know why we native West Coasters are so passive-aggressive. Anytime I'm around Lowell and observe his direct way of speaking, direct line of questioning, and direct style of writing, I admire how much better it is than the rest of ours.

I was super lucky to call Lowell a colleague from 1995 to 1999 when we were both at the *Santa Rosa Press Democrat*. I never had a colleague like Lowell before. You could go to dinner with Lowell and talk about Floyd Patterson, Kafka, and Woody Allen. Not necessarily in that order. Sometimes in that order, though.

I'd read Lowell and be in awe. Why didn't I write as cleanly as he did? Why were my sentences so much longer and more cluttered than Lowell's? How did Lowell observe that motivation in that coach's behavior, when all I did was transcribe the quote?

Lowell is a thinker. That PhD didn't fall off a tree, even though he got it at Stanford, where there are lots of trees. But you'd never meet a less-stuffy guy with a literature doctorate than Lowell Cohn. That's what makes Lowell's writing so great. Take a big brain that's read all the great books, add in an innate passion for sports, combine it with a keen eye on human behavior, and then dip it all in a big vat of Brooklyn *getouttaheah* humor. You don't get combo platters like that.

This memoir is loaded with funny stuff. Hilarious stories about Al Davis and Frank Robinson and Will Clark and the Brooklyn playgrounds of his youth. That's another thing about Lowell. How long he gifted us with his writing. The stories span from how he learned to be tough from "the Sals" on a Brooklyn playground in the 1950s to living in a world where breaking the story of Walsh's leukemia diagnosis happened in a modern media split second.

And the stories are the best. Lowell may have been so savage in some of his blunt observations that he tells us he was known as "that asshole" by many of his peers, but that also means that when Lowell tells us an emotional story, the impact is that much greater. With Lowell, the toughness of his prose buys him the kind of credibility that allows for a wallop of feeling when he lets you inside, like he does when he tells you the story about his dad taking him to a baseball game when he was a kid.

I grew up reading *Sports Illustrated* and fell in love with the long-form poetry of Frank Deford and Gary Smith. I thought I was supposed to try to make everything an epic poem. And then I read Lowell and realized you earn so much more with the reader by stripping it down. Lowell eschews flowery language. I once asked him why he was so in love with boxing. He told me, "because it's basic. And basic is the best drama." That's his writing. If illustrating basic themes of the human experience was a good enough road map for a guy like Shakespeare, it was good enough for a Jewish kid from Brooklyn who saw all those themes on display when watching *Friday Night Fights*.

I should probably get going, so you can read the memoir. You'll see what I mean. You'll read how he is open-minded, even apologizing to a guy he thinks is a lowlife, like Billy Martin. Or how he doesn't buy the politically correct line of turning Colin Kaepernick into Muhammad Ali. Or how he gleans the deepest of meanings from the most basic of interactions. I'm thinking about his story of Billy Beane and Brian Sabean and their offices. Or how an afternoon with *Peanuts* creator Charles Schulz made time stand still.

Lowell's career was so rich, he got to sit next to Red Smith at the 1981 World Series. If you don't know who Red Smith is, you probably should. Lowell asked him what to do when a column didn't come to him on deadline. Red Smith, because he's Red Smith, told Lowell, "The Lord provides."

In the end, that's what reading Lowell's memoir made me think. I devoured the thing. I laughed. I got emotional. I learned a lot about sports and life. And I thought: how lucky are we that we get to read Lowell again?

The Lord provided.

INTRODUCTION

WHEN I BEGAN AS A SPORTS COLUMNIST IN 1979, my name was That Asshole.

It's what most San Francisco Bay Area sports writers called me, and I understood why. I had jumped the queue. Most had studied journalism in college and started out covering high school sports and diligently worked their way through the system to become a beat writer or feature writer or columnist. It was orderly and it made sense, and then I came along, having done none of the standard things, and became an instant columnist. I made a mockery of the system, destroyed it—an asshole. If I met someone like me, I'd consider him an asshole, too.

I never studied journalism. I never covered high school sports. After graduate school studying English literature at Stanford, I began as a freelance film critic in California at the *Palo Alto Times*, now defunct. The *Times* paid me ten bucks a review—this was in the 1970s. I was thrilled to get it. After my first year, the editor phoned me, said he was giving me a 25 percent raise—that's how strong my reviews were. Now I was making twelve-fifty a pop.

I sold a few articles to *Sports Illustrated* and, in a moment of mad chutzpah, sent them to the *San Francisco Chronicle*. The managing editor wrote back, said if ever I was in the neighborhood, I should drop by. I wrote back, said I lived thirty-five miles away in Palo Alto, certainly in the neighborhood. We made an appointment and he hired me as a columnist because my background was *not* in sports journalism. He wanted me to write as an outsider with fresh eyes. That was the theory.

In my first column I questioned why teams played the national anthem before games, said professional sports had zero to do with patriotism. This was decades before Colin Kaepernick and other athletes started kneeling for the anthem. Readers went nuts with outrage, just what the *Chronicle* wanted.

I wrote that the Oakland Raiders didn't look so tough out of their uniforms, many with fat, unathletic bodies. One with a pencil neck. Schlubs. It pissed off the Raiders and readers. But it was a different look at sports. I compared Muhammad Ali to Beowulf. Not one of my best.

Sports people didn't know what to make of me. I asked about their haircuts or what they read or ate. I wrote why white guys and black guys had trouble performing smooth handshakes. I had never learned the maneuvers African Americans used with each other, and when I shook hands with a black player our hands collided. We were speaking two different languages—or shaking hands in different grammars. These were topics that didn't seem to be about sports. I wrote in scenes, tried to make characters come alive, used dialogue, created dramatic tension.

I also took controversial stands, criticized local teams when they deserved it. Not the norm in the Bay Area, where sports writers were considered soft, especially compared to the blunt, plainspoken, in-your-face style of New York City, where I was from and where I learned to think and talk and write.

I took strong stands because that's just how I was. And I needed to make a splash. Needed to keep my job. I was on a six-month trial, and if I were mere background noise, the *Chronicle* would drop me in a second.

Readers hated me, but they read me. Made assumptions about what I was like without ever meeting me. That felt weird, but on the other hand, I got to see my face on the sides of buses around town, an ad campaign the *Chronicle* ran for me. Strange to see my puss on a bus, but kind of a rush, too.

Being inside the hurricane like that was a blast. I had been trained as an academic, a world with no action. No action in the deathly still library filled with dust motes floating in half-light, or a polite, earnest graduate seminar in Henry James. But sports writing was pure action. I needed action, craved it. And I needed the gratification of seeing my article in the paper the next day.

After years on the job, I established my bona fides. I became just plain Lowell Cohn to the other writers and players. No longer That Asshole. I think.

What follows is a collection of stories about the famous people I met, the strange things they did—a behind-the-scenes look at what they were really like. Observing them, being near them, I sometimes clasped my hand over my mouth in sheer astonishment at the varieties of human behavior. Some disturbing, others wonderful. Most of these stories I have never told. They appear in no particular order and end in 2017, when I retired after nearly forty years on the job.

GLOVES OFF

40 Years of Unfiltered Sports Writing

THE ESSAYS

BREAKING NEWS:
BILL WALSH IS DYING

IN THE FALL OF 2006, BILL WALSH WAS DYING. Ira Miller, my colleague when I worked at the *San Francisco Chronicle*, and I were the only sports writers who knew. We had covered Bill's career as coach of the 49ers, and he'd recently told us he had leukemia.

But he asked us not to write it, and we didn't. This was Bill's life—and eventually his death—and he, not us, was in charge of breaking the news in his own time, at his own pace. People assume journalists are heartless, would commit homicide for a scoop. Sometimes, you judge journalists by the stories they don't write.

I was in Seattle later that fall, eating dinner with some sports writers the night before a 49ers-Seahawks game. My cell phone rang. It was Ira Miller and he wanted to know if I was alone, his voice insistent. I said I was with writers. He ordered me immediately to walk outside the restaurant, talk to him on the street. He said writers are nosy and they're smart and they'd figure out what we were talking about. Figure it out fast.

I walked outside, said I was alone. Didn't know why Ira called. Ira said he was phoning from the press box of the Oakland Coliseum, where he was covering a Raiders game, but now he was alone in a hallway.

"What's going on?" I asked.

"The writers from the *Contra Costa Times* know something about Bill," Ira said. Whispering now. "I heard them say he's ill. They're talking about writing a story. You better tell Bill."

I walked back into the restaurant, said I had to leave, dropped money on the table, walked out. The writers stared at me. They knew something was up, wondered if I'd beaten them on something. It's how journalists are, their feelers always waving in the air.

I phoned Bill from my hotel room, my voice tense. Told him the *Contra Costa Times* knew something, but I wasn't sure what. Ira had heard them talking in the press box. Bill was silent a long time. When he spoke, I expected him to be nervous—often he was a nervous, fretful man. But he spoke in the voice of a leader, of a great head coach.

"I'm not worried about the *Contra Costa Times*," he said. "They haven't phoned me. They don't know anything. If they call, I'll know how to handle it."

"Okay, Bill," I said. "Ira and I didn't want you to get caught by surprise." Me talking to a man about his life, his life in my hands.

"We're okay, Lowell," Bill said. "Thanks for letting me know."

*****

And that was that until a few weeks later, when I was driving to the Sonoma Coast with my wife. I was taking a few days off from my job writing sports columns for the *Santa Rosa Press Democrat* and had rented a house on a cliff overlooking the Pacific, needing the peace of the breaking waves and the salt-sweet air. My phone rang somewhere past the town of Jenner on the narrow, winding Pacific Coast Highway.

"Lowell, it's Bill." Nervous now. Definitely nervous.

"Word's getting out," he said. He sighed, a deep life-sigh. "People are beginning to call me. I want you and Ira to break the news."

Because he was an old-time coach, he was faithful to the older writers who'd put in their time. A pro seeking out pros. And he trusted us to do it right.

That's what I think, what I'd like to think. But I couldn't talk then. A moment like this arrives, a dying man calling me, and I'm temporarily in limbo. I said, embarrassed, "Bill, I'm driving up to Sea Ranch. I can't do this now. I still have a ways to go and Ira is in LA."

I couldn't believe I was saying this—to a man facing the ultimate.

"Can you set it up for tomorrow morning?" he said, frustrated, needing to get it over with.

Next morning, we had a three-way phone conversation, call it a conference call about Bill's disease. He asked us to write he had leukemia. "Please write it," he said.

About small things, Bill Walsh could be petty. This was known. And he could be a whiner. This also was known. But now he was brave and forceful, and I was getting a lesson in the proper way to conduct myself in the inevitable crisis, the proper way to prepare for . . . well, God knows what.

We talked for forty-five minutes, Bill, Ira, and I, Bill going over the details with the same care he took in creating his game plans. He told us that two years earlier, doctors discovered he was anemic. "When they tested the bone marrow, they found I was deficient," he said.

But it was way more than anemia.

He'd recently had a series of transfusions and said he was feeling better. "I'm positive, but not evangelistic," he told us. "I'm pragmatically doing everything my physicians recommend, and I'm working my way through it."

Walsh already had let former players know—news to us. He said about a hundred had called. He had recently had breakfast with quarterback Joe Montana, the most famous player Walsh ever drafted and developed. Walsh had talked several times on the phone with Steve Young, another 49ers Hall of Fame quarterback, and they were trying to set up a meeting. Jerry Rice, Keena Turner, and Ronnie Lott had been especially helpful.

Former 49ers owner Eddie DeBartolo Jr. recently flew from his home in Florida to visit Walsh. There had been trouble between the two men, especially after DeBartolo stripped Walsh of his title as 49ers president. But they had made up years ago, and the previous summer Walsh had attended a lavish party in Las Vegas DeBartolo threw for former 49ers players and coaches.

"News about me has been circulating," Walsh told us. "It's been getting back to me. There are too many people following the progress of this. I felt it was appropriate to confirm what's happening."

Walsh was quiet a while. We could hear him breathing hard over the phone.

"I'm running out of energy," he admitted, his voice stripped of life. "Did you get what you need?"

We said we had.

After Bill hung up, Ira and I, writing for different publications, went over the basic facts with each other. Then we made a pact. We would file our stories at exactly the same moment—we checked our watches. Forget about who got credit for breaking the story. Who cared who got credit?

I sent the story to my paper and phoned my editor, who said, "You're on vacation. Why are you calling?"

I told him Bill Walsh had leukemia and I had just sent him the story breaking the news.

"No shit." He was awestruck. This was Bill Walsh and our paper had the story. He said he'd read the story and phone me right back. Called back in two minutes.

"Holy shit," he said.

He thanked me and said I handled it right—I was a columnist and rarely wrote news stories. And then he said he'd send the story to the Associated Press for national dissemination. This was a big deal and AP needed it, he said.

Twenty minutes later—it couldn't have been more—my wife and I were eating lunch, ham-and-cheese sandwiches and Knorr cream of leek soup, something I never eat except at the chilly, windy Sonoma Coast where it makes me feel warm and secure. My wife turned on the TV to CNN, or it could have been ESPN. An announcer said this bulletin just in: Bill Walsh revealed he has leukemia. The announcer told a few more details.

My wife, who is not a journalist, stared at me, eyes wide.

"How in the world did that story go from this kitchen, on this deserted coast, to TV so fast? How did that happen?"

I told her that was modern media. News travels at the speed of light, even from here with just us, the sea lions, and a few foxes. I could see she was impressed.

I put on a warm jacket and walked south along the cliff overlooking the moving, agitated sea, the water the only sound except for seabirds. I walked past a Monterey cypress giving me shade, walked with my head down. Not long ago, I remembered, Bill and I had talked on the phone. When I got ready to hang up, he said, "I've enjoyed our intellectual conversations," meaning they soon would end.

"Screw intellectual, Bill," I said. "I like you."

MAYO ON THE SIDE:
BILL WALSH DIES

B ILL WALSH WANTED THE MORTADELLA SANDWICH. Ira Miller and I had
driven to Walsh's home in Woodside, California, an upscale suburb of
San Francisco. It was 2007 and Walsh had acknowledged to the world
he had leukemia. Ira and I wanted to see him. See how he was doing. We had
covered his entire tenure with the 49ers, his epic career transforming the 49ers
into a legendary franchise, winning three Super Bowls, developing Joe Montana, Jerry Rice, and Steve Young. We knew him better than any other sports
personality, and now that we no longer covered him, now that the battles were
over, we cared for him deeply.

When we arrived at his house, the huge gate was open. We drove into the
parking lot, walked to the front door, and rang the bell. No answer. We definitely had a lunch date with Walsh. We walked back to the car, and now the
gate was closed. A gardener, it seemed, had finished his work and driven off,

and we were locked in. Looked like a couple of second-story men.

Ira phoned Walsh at Stanford where he kept an office and said we were at his house. Over the cell phone, I heard Walsh say, "Oh!" He had forgotten. Nothing new with him. He forgot things all the time. A few months earlier, he had invited me to lunch at a place across the street from Stanford. I was sitting at a table waiting when my phone rang. Walsh's administrative assistant. She asked if Bill and I had scheduled lunch. I said, yes, I was at the restaurant. She said Bill forgot but would be there in five minutes. He arrived embarrassed, and then he did something he never did. Put his arm around my shoulder. He did not like to touch people. Or people to touch him. I knew something must be up. Did not know the something was leukemia.

His forgetfulness applied to his car, whichever car it was on any given day. He would leave his car with the door locked but the key in the ignition and the engine running. Happened all the time. And he'd wait, embarrassed, for the AAA truck and the driver to unlock his car. And he lost wallets by the ton.

He was an absentminded professor. Absentminded doesn't mean vacant-minded. On the contrary. It means someone so intensely focused on one thing he forgets other things, peripheral things. That was Walsh. When he was a coach, he thought about offense, the beauty of making plays, the sheer choreography of it. Now, he was thinking about life and death.

He immediately drove from Stanford to his home for lunch with Ira and me. He unlocked the gate, parked his car next to ours, and took us around to the backyard deck with picnic umbrellas, the deck abutting a chardonnay vineyard. Walsh was not a red wine drinker. He drank California chardonnay—I believe the tannins in red wine gave him a headache. The pretext for our lunch was a half-case of chardonnay from Jack Cakebread who owned Cakebread Cellars in Napa, producing world-class wines. Jack Cakebread was a superstar in the wine world, but when it comes to sports celebrities, famous people turn shy. Cakebread wouldn't dare approach Walsh himself with his wine. He asked me to bring it.

Walsh chose a bottle and opened it and we drank, Walsh, Ira, and I, the golden liquid perfect, the three of us getting buzzed at one o'clock in the afternoon. Walsh saw the three sandwiches I had brought—roast beef, turkey, and mortadella. "Could I have the mortadella?" he asked.

It was amazing we were having this lunch at all. I had published a book about Walsh's return to Stanford for his second stint as head football coach in 1992, and Walsh didn't like the book when it appeared. He had given me full access but didn't understand what that meant. It meant he didn't control how I portrayed him. I believe I made him an admirable character, heroic at times. But he wasn't satisfied. I narrated scenes when he said *fuck*. Nothing unusual in that.

Follow the syllogism: All football coaches say fuck. Walsh was a football coach. Walsh said fuck.

He said it all the time. Sometimes every other sentence. *Where's the fucking running back? What the fuck happened on that play?* Fuck was an indispensable part of his lexicon. His use of fuck humanized him, made me like him, would help readers relate to him as a regular guy instead of a starry-eyed genius. But he was image-obsessed. If he said fuck, what would people think of him?

They'd think he said fuck like everyone else.

He was fucking sore at me about fuck.

Also sore about what I quoted him saying, especially about Stanford's opponents. He put down Northwestern, said the Wildcats were a sorry outfit. Which they were. Northwestern was offended. Walsh never liked people being angry at him. Had a horror of direct confrontation. Held Northwestern against me.

When my book came out, Walsh went on national television and, with a grief-stricken face, said, "This book that's been written I had nothing to do with." An interesting statement considering we had signed a contract giving him a healthy part of my advance from HarperCollins. Sure seemed like he had something to do with the book. He had said he would donate his share of the advance to Stanford athletics. I believe he did, although I never checked. If he wanted nothing to do with the advance, I sure could have used the money. I reminded him he had signed a contract. I told him not to deny it again. He said he understood. I could not give up my anger. He made me look bad on television and he bad-mouthed me to his coaches.

We did not speak for years after that. I didn't want to. One time in the late 1990s, Walsh attended a 49ers practice. Walsh was not associated with the team then, although he would come back later. He walked over to me and made small talk, complained he ran into traffic on the drive down. I pointed to the 49ers beat writer for the *Santa Rosa Press Democrat*, a young man named Brian Murphy. I told Walsh that Murphy was interesting. Walsh said hello to him. I walked away. Later, Murphy said to me, "I can't believe you handed off Bill Walsh to me."

Walsh wanted to be friends with me—whatever that meant—but I rejected him. This seems astonishing to me now. But there it was. I rejected Bill Walsh.

Walsh and I had been close before the book appeared. He was an endearing man with a warm, lovely smile. He was brilliant and funny, had mastered irony, had great comic timing.

And he was capable of acts of kindness. His defensive coordinator during his second tenure at Stanford was Fred vonAppen, who also had coached with Walsh during Walsh's first go-round at Stanford in 1977 and 1978. In 1980, vonAppen was an assistant coach for the Packers but quit during the season over a dispute with management. Walsh understood vonAppen, saw him as a man of deeply held principles who sometimes allowed his principles to impede his self-preservation. Walsh was afraid the NFL would blackball vonAppen. Walsh phoned vonAppen in Green Bay and said he wanted vonAppen to check out hot college prospects in Wisconsin. VonAppen always believed the scouting position was a put-up job, pure busywork. The 49ers already had scouts assigned to the Midwest. That didn't matter to Walsh. He had saved vonAppen, placed vonAppen under his protection. From that moment on, vonAppen pledged to Walsh his unconditional loyalty.

Walsh always could relate to an underdog. His father had been abusive to him, and Walsh felt an endless need for encouragement and psychological hand-holding. He had a horror of people being angry with him.

While I was researching the book—this would have been 1992—Walsh said something that inflamed NFL coach Don Shula. I don't remember what. Shula wrote Walsh an angry letter. I was surprised at Shula's language. It indicated to me an animosity that might have gone back years. Walsh's hands shook as he handed me the letter.

"What should I do?" he asked after I read it. He sounded like a scolded child.

I told him to send Shula a case of wine.

"I also need to write him a letter," Walsh said. "Would you write it for me?"

Hell, yes.

I wrote a polite, diplomatic, self-effacing, sincere letter. Walsh read it. Walsh liked it. Walsh mailed it and Shula was appeased. Shula later came to Walsh's memorial service, one great coach honoring another, one friend there for an old friend. I saw that, and was proud I came through for Walsh.

Walsh was a confessional man, needed to get things off his chest, an endless list of things. During that 1992 season I spent with him at Stanford, he told me things. We would have a drink at Rickey's Hyatt House on El Camino Real in

Palo Alto the night before Stanford home games. One night, former Redskins coach Joe Gibbs was in the bar. Gibbs' son Coy played on Walsh's team. When we walked into the bar, Gibbs was walking out. As Gibbs and Walsh passed each other, they nodded. Just nodded. Not a single word.

"What was that, Bill?" I asked.

"We were rivals," he said. That was all. They had been rivals. Who knew what went on? So much of Walsh was the dark side of the moon.

Walsh defined friendship a certain way. A friend was someone who listened to him. He was not interested in listening to you or me. I accepted that. He once told me he and his wife, Geri, were staying at Lake Tahoe. He was driving back to their place from the store, and the car behind was crowding him. The driver became aggressive. Walsh pulled over to the side of the road. Signaled for the other guy to pull over. The guy pulled over. They stood facing each other in the white snow. Walsh put up his fists. Motioned to the guy. The guy walked forward. Walsh punched him hard several times in the face—he had boxed at San Jose State, was handy with his fists. The guy fell down in the snow, red with his blood. Walsh drove off, proud he had knocked out a young punk trying to take advantage of an older man. When he got home, Geri asked why he had blood on his shirt. Walsh didn't explain.

This he told me at Rickey's one Friday night. Another time, he was depressed because his Stanford Cardinal team was losing games and he saw no hope. This was in 1993 and they would finish the season 4-7, a blow to Walsh's image and ego. He sat at a table in the bar drinking a margarita. It was getting late and I said I needed to drive home. He said he'd see me at the game on Saturday and I left the bar. I walked through the lobby, along a hallway which led to the deserted parking lot. In the parking lot I heard someone behind me, got the shaky feeling I experience walking down dark empty streets in New York. I thought a mugger was following me. I walked faster. I was nearly at my car. The person was on me now.

I whipped my head around.

Walsh.

"Do you think we can win tomorrow?" His voice pleading.

He was asking a sports writer?

"Yes, Bill. I feel sure you'll win."

"Really?"

"Oh, yes. I'm certain."

"Good, I'm glad you feel that way," he said, reassured.

Stanford got its ass kicked.

*****

But that was long in the past. In 1999, the 49ers brought Walsh back as vice president and general manager. That created a problem. A columnist has to do business with the general manager, and Walsh and I were barely grunting at each other. My wife told me to make it right. I phoned Walsh's office at the 49ers headquarters, spoke to his administrative assistant Jane Walsh (no relation), and asked for an appointment. She gave me a time slot at lunchtime the next day. I made the drive to Santa Clara feeling uneasy. What would this be like?

I entered the high-ceilinged lobby, a football cathedral. Reporters milled about. What was this? Someone said Walsh was going to talk to the group. I had been relegated to one of the mob. Walsh appeared at the top of the stairs. Big grin. White hair perfectly coiffed. Handsome. He allowed reporters to shout questions up the stairs to him. He answered like Caesar dispensing crumbs to the rabble. This was it? Reporters competed for his attention. I got ready to walk out the door.

"I have an appointment," I heard Walsh announce. "Lowell, can you come up here?"

Everyone else hated my guts. I would have hated my guts if I were them. I walked up the wide, tall staircase, enjoying a petty victory. Sometimes petty victories are the best. Walsh led me into his office. He didn't sit behind his desk. We sat across from each other at a small table. I interviewed him about something or other, but the subject didn't matter. The real subject was the act of talking, of looking each other in the eye. Finally, Walsh said, "Are you done?" I said I was done. I stood up to leave.

"Don't go," he said.

Jane Walsh wheeled a table into the room. On the table were sandwiches and soft drinks.

"Have lunch with me," Walsh said.

This was a peace offering. He was a bigger man than I was. We ate lunch. We talked. We reestablished our connection, returned to where we had been. He would talk about himself and I would listen. Okay, I'd be a listener.

And after that, the circle closed. We talked constantly.

He taught a class at Stanford's Graduate School of Business, and he thought his voice sounded weak, that he was no longer a commanding presence. He told me this on the phone. I said his voice was just fine. That didn't satisfy him. He said he was shaky on the subject matter. I said the students were there to imbibe the Walshness of Bill Walsh. He was the subject matter. That made him feel better. He was always looking to feel better. He started every day of his life with a deficit. I never understood why.

He would phone me complaining about John York who ran the 49ers with his wife, Denise—this was before their son Jed York took over. Walsh didn't like York. Thought he was cheap and small-minded. I once told Walsh I had dinner with York and had a good time. Walsh sighed into the phone.

"He would enjoy your conversation," he told me, "but you wouldn't want to work for him."

After Walsh stepped down as general manager and now was merely called a 49ers "consultant," he called me at home. This would have been 2001. Walsh's voice shook. He said York had humiliated him. *Humiliated* was the word he used. It was about a car. Walsh was talking so fast I had trouble keeping up. Something about York inviting him to lunch and asking if he still drove a 49ers car, and Walsh saying yes, and York saying he no longer deserved a 49ers car.

"He could have asked a secretary to phone me," Walsh said. "You don't invite me to lunch for that. He humiliated me."

I never understood the car issue. If it even happened. Or what it meant. But Walsh was beside himself.

Or he would call about the Oakland Raiders. Walsh always would bring up Raiders defensive coordinator Rob Ryan, whom he called a fat fuck. Ryan's gut preceded him by a half foot and hung over his belt like a water bag. His gray hair was long and uncombed and, all in all, he looked like he had crawled out of the hamper. Walsh had disdain for fat people. He was trim, worked hard to look good, and he insisted his coaches keep fit, cut an athletic image. Walsh constantly phoned Davis about Ryan and said, "You've got to fire that fat motherfucker."

One day Walsh phoned me in 2006. His voice was soft and I heard strange noises in the background.

"Where are you, Bill?" I asked.

"Stanford Hospital."

"What are you doing there?"

"Just here for some tests."

"Tests?"

"They're checking something."

"What are they checking?"

"My blood."

His blood?

*****

And now we were sitting in his backyard in 2007 with a Cakebread chardonnay and he was eating the mortadella because his wife, Geri, was of Italian descent and she cooked Italian and he loved mortadella. He looked at me and pointed to his mouth. I didn't know what he meant. He did it again, pointed to his mouth and then pointed at me.

"You have mayonnaise on your lip," he said.

I was eating the turkey and I got mayo on my lip. I wiped it off. I still think about Walsh and the mayonnaise because it's one of the last things we ever spoke about. Mayonnaise.

Why was he pointing out the mayo? Was he doing me a favor because anyone would look like a doofus with a glob of mayo on the lip? Was he doing it for himself, because who wants to stare at a person with a white dollop on the corner of his mouth? Or did Walsh merely want things right? He had a rage for order.

Years before, he once walked through the 49ers headquarters and noticed framed photos and artwork were at willy-nilly angles on the wall. He was appalled at such carelessness. He went around the building straightening the picture frames and then had them bolted into place. Players and coaches couldn't help noticing the head custodian was gone a few days later.

In the locker room, Walsh always lined up his shoes perfectly in front of his cubicle, his socks neatly folded into each shoe. He demanded absolute precision from his players. His offensive game plans were works of art. Coaches do not write Xs and Os. They write Os and triangles. Walsh's Os and triangles were beautiful. Someone could frame them for an art gallery. A man with that sensibility would find misplaced mayo irredeemably inelegant. So, I remember the mayonnaise and it makes me smile.

After a while, Walsh began to fade. Ira and I saw him tiring and we started to leave. He asked us to gather the plates and glasses and carry them to the kitchen. He asked us to place the scraps in the garbage under the sink. He asked us to rinse the dishes and put them in the dishwasher.

"Geri likes a neat house," he said.

He wearily walked us to the door.

"So long, men," he said.

Not so long, Lowell and Ira. So long, men. He would call his players men during practice, but we weren't his players. He was pulling back from us, making things formal.

"We will never see Bill again," I told Ira as we drove away.

"Why do you say that?"

"Because he just said goodbye forever."

Six weeks later, on July 30, 2007, Bill Walsh died.

03

RIVALRY: AL DAVIS MISSES
BILL WALSH, SORT OF

O AKLAND RAIDERS OWNER AL DAVIS shuffled into the room. He wore white Reeboks and the white version of his Raiders outfit, which made him look like a male nurse or the Good Humor Man. In his younger days, he had worn black patent-leather loafers with a gold strap across the top. He'd loudly scraped his heels on the floor emphasizing his approach, announcing that he'd arrived.

But those days were behind him. He was emaciated and his outfit hung loosely on him like a suit too big for its wire hanger. Open sores, partly hidden by Band-Aids, covered his face. His skin was translucent, his cheeks sunken. He was in his late seventies and his body was breaking down. It had been a fine body, nurtured by frequent weight lifting and good eating. But it was betraying him and he would openly complain that, although he had dominated most things in his life, he could not dominate death. *Dominate* was a significant word in his lexicon along with *cocksucker*. In four years, he'd be dead.

But today wasn't about his death. It was about Bill Walsh's death. Walsh, the genius behind the 49ers, had died a few days earlier from leukemia. Davis was sore at Walsh for not fighting harder against death. He would tell reporters, tell anyone, that Walsh—who finally refused treatment, who didn't want to live a life that was no life—gave up too soon. "Bill was preparing for something that I thought could be forestalled," Davis said. Davis would have fought like hell.

Davis and Walsh had a complicated relationship. Davis gave Walsh his start in the NFL in 1966 as an assistant coach, but after one year Walsh asked for a $10,000 raise and Davis refused. So Walsh was reduced to coaching the San Jose Apaches, a minor-league team. In years to come, Davis would rub the Apaches in Walsh's face, saying the guy across the Bay (San Francisco) had coached a minor-league outfit. This burned up Walsh, who had a fragile ego and held grudges.

Walsh outshone Davis, especially in the Bay Area, because Davis moved the Raiders to Los Angeles. Walsh changed offense in the league and Davis never did anything like that. Davis was jealous of Walsh. Davis was a tough guy, said things like "who the fuck asked you." Walsh had better manners and, although he was a coach and said fuck every other sentence, he shied away from direct confrontation, from arguing. Walsh admired Davis' willingness to be crude. He was also appalled by it. He once told me he and Davis were having dinner at a fancy place and some fan, an older man slightly drunk, walked over to them. Said it was amazing to see these two giants of football together. Davis and Walsh shook his hand, but the man didn't leave. He was grooving on being near them.

"Did you get what you need?" Davis finally asked.

"Yes," the fan said.

"Then get the fuck out of here."

Walsh laughed telling me that story. He admired the way Davis acted and he didn't admire it. He admired that Davis took no shit. But in certain ways, Davis was a phony. He wanted people to believe he had been a first-rate athlete. Walsh was never outstanding but he boxed and played wide receiver at San Jose State. Davis never even rose to that level. He was a reasonable junior-varsity athlete in basketball and football, never more than that. Yet, in high school and college at Syracuse he managed to insert himself into the team photos. He was Zelig. He hung around with the real athletes, created the illusion he was one of them.

He was a talented actor. Even in the way he spoke. He was pure Brooklyn, would lapse into "dese" and "dose." Then, in the twinkling of an eye, he'd sound

Southern, talk about the greatness of the Raiders, softening the final "ers," saying Rai-dahhhhhhhhhhs. He'd use a rising inflection at the end. When he went pure Southern, he routinely elongated two-syllable words into four syllables.

As a young man, he was assistant football coach at the Citadel in South Carolina, and he latched onto a Southern drawl the way some people latch onto a style of dressing. He might go from Brooklyn speech to Southern speech, or vice versa, in a single sentence. Could start with a dependent clause in Brooklyn, and handle the independent clause sounding like Colonel Sanders. In between words, he'd splice in loads of *umm, umm, umms*, and he'd suck his teeth and, listening to him, you wanted to say, "Get to the point, will you?" Another sports columnist familiar with Davis said when Davis went into his Southern accent you knew he was lying. I didn't find it that simple. Davis could lie or tell the truth in many dialects.

Walsh made fun of Davis, although Davis never knew. When Walsh was dying and rarely left the house, he made phone calls. I was on the phone tree. He would call me, his voice frail, his life fleeing. He mostly wanted to talk about the Raiders. They were awful, were coming off a 2-14 season, and this pleased Walsh. The Raiders and 49ers had been rivals and that explains part of it. But there was more. There was Davis. Walsh enjoyed seeing him down, would laugh about him and his team. But he also respected Davis. Conflicted to the very end. A few weeks before he died, Walsh attended a Raiders practice. This made Davis proud. I believe Davis' feelings for Walsh ran deeper than Walsh's for Davis. After Walsh died, Davis suggested someone name a quarterback award after Walsh. Davis called Walsh's death a "devastation."

*****

So, Davis shuffled into a large conference room in Napa at high noon, July 2007. The Napa Marriott where the Raiders held their preseason camp. He saw me and winced. Disappointed in me. Forever disappointed. I criticized him and his team. I wasn't loyal. Although loyalty is not a relevant concept for a journalist, loyalty was big with Davis. And he didn't like that I called him "Al." Most of the media called him Mr. Davis, a man with a title. But I had called Bill Walsh "Bill" and Carmen Policy "Carmen" and Eddie DeBartolo Jr. "Eddie" and they didn't take offense, so what was this "Mr. Davis" stuff?

And there was something else. Al felt I had betrayed him. We were two Jewish guys from Flatbush, Brooklyn. We knew each other's neighborhoods and we were quintessentially Brooklyn, yet we had never been close. From his point of view, my fault.

He had attended Erasmus Hall High School on Flatbush Avenue near Church Avenue. I went to Midwood on Bedford Avenue near Glenwood Road. Rival schools. Erasmus started in 1786, was the first secondary school the New York State Board of Regents chartered. Its list of attendees is startling: Bobby Fischer, Bernard Malamud, Barbra Streisand, Bob Arum, Clara Bow, Billy Cunningham, Jerry Reinsdorf, Beverly Sills, Mickey Spillane, Barbara Stanwyck, Eli Wallach, Mae West.

At Midwood we had Woody Allen. Period. Oh, there was Erich Segal, who wrote *Love Story*, if he counts.

Erasmus was the school with the rich history and Al knew it. As he carefully made his way into the conference room, he said, "Lowell Cohn," his tone acid.

"Hi, Al," I said.

He proceeded to inform me and everyone in the room that he had recently been with Bill Walsh, at Walsh's deathbed, keeping the death vigil. And he had told Walsh he finally figured out why Lowell Cohn doesn't like him.

Walsh asked why.

"Because my high school always kicked his high school's ass in football."

I stared at Al. Was he serious?

Here are the problems I have with Al's story.

He really, honestly, sincerely talked to Walsh about me and Midwood High School football with Walsh just hours away from death? Doubtful.

And Walsh, who was about to meet his maker or go to heaven or solve life's greatest mystery, was actually interested in the Midwood-Erasmus rivalry— two schools he knew nothing about? This was what Walsh's life came down to, Midwood-Erasmus, his Rosebud?

Al expected me, a man in his sixties at the time, someone who had lived in California more than forty years, to care about Erasmus kicking Midwood's ass. For real?

I told Al it obviously made him happy that Erasmus beat Midwood and I was glad for him. Not that I meant it. Al seemed pleased.

Out of curiosity, I looked up the Midwood-Erasmus rivalry in my three years at Midwood. For some reason, I couldn't find the scores, but I found Erasmus' record: 0–6 in 1959, 2–5 in 1960, and 3–4 in 1961, so Erasmus wasn't kicking anyone's ass back then.

Neither was Al in 2007 or after.

I have thought about that day over the years. Thought about what Al did, what he really did. He had called a news conference to talk about Walsh's death, the death of a great man in his world and in the entire sports world. But Al made the day about himself, something he always managed to do. Walsh, who was the center of the story, moved to the periphery in Al's narration to us. It was all about Al: Al had been on Walsh's deathwatch; Al encouraged Walsh to fight harder against death; Al got credit for being the loyal friend; Al had initiated the conversation about high school football, which clearly was about him and not about Walsh. Walsh, the dying man, became Al's audience. Al was the star in the story of Walsh's life and death, and Walsh became a supporting character.

Al already was suffering from muscular degeneration, which would kill him. He told us the condition was minor. He was lying to himself. Walsh's death frightened him. "My contemporaries are just leaving me," Al often said in a sad voice. That was the real meaning of his speech that day. He was scared for himself. As he stared at me and talked nonsense about high school, talked about kicking Midwood's ass and by implication my ass, he knew the truth. He would never kick death's ass. Walsh had proved that. Al looked into the room of reporters and saw his train coming, coming toward him, saw his name and death date inscribed on the locomotive, saw it roaring down the track.

CATTLE: BARRY BONDS
USES A BAT IN AN
UNUSUAL WAY

B ARRY BONDS WAS THE SADDEST ATHLETE I EVER COVERED. He should
have been happy because he had everything. He was good-looking, had
a warm smile, could be endearing, and he was a great baseball player.
San Francisco Giants Hall of Famer Orlando Cepeda told me Bonds had the
best swing of anyone he ever saw, and Cepeda had played with Willie Mays.

But Bonds was uncomfortable. In every way you can imagine. He was uncomfortable with himself, with his teammates, with the media. He was a cloud
in the room, relentlessly rude. He was arrogant. One person in the Giants ad-
ministration told Bonds, "When you're done, you'll end up like the fool on the
hill, all alone."

Bonds even forgot the name of Giants general manager Brian Sabean on
at least one occasion. He was somehow above mere names. Bonds' teammates
knew he was an asshole, but they liked him. Or felt neutral about him. He

was not a high-maintenance teammate, kept to himself. Giants shortstop Rich Aurilia once told me, "Guys complained Barry didn't do team stretching before games. What did I care about him doing team stretching? He was Barry Bonds. He helped us win."

When he was drug-engorged, when he hit seventy-three home runs in 2001, he became so big he didn't actually run. You couldn't call it running. He navigated his bulk, steered it like an ocean liner approaching port. It was horrible to see. I once wrote an entire column about him without mentioning his name. I called him *It*. He had become a chemical thing. Readers knew whom I meant. He never admitted to knowingly taking performance-enhancing drugs, said he took them unwittingly.

Seriously?

In 2011, a US District Court in San Francisco tried and convicted him for obstruction of justice—the guilty verdict got overturned. I covered that trial, sat right behind Bonds' mother, Pat. Every morning, Bonds would arrive in court in a neat, dark suit—he had lost weight, was trim and looked normal. He would see his mother and in the gentlest voice say, "Hi, Mom." And I wished I had met that Barry, the one capable of saying *Hi, Mom*, the one wanting to get along.

His last season with the Giants was 2007—it was his last season in baseball. After 2007, no team signed him. I covered spring training in 2007, and after the fifth inning of one game, the Giants public-relations staff announced Bonds was coming out of the lineup and would be available at his locker.

I need to explain the protocol of spring training, different from the regular season. In a regular-season game, the media waits until after the game to interview the manager and players. Not so in spring training, where everything is casual and teams bend the rules. In spring training, the star players often leave the game early, actually leave the ballpark. Some go home, some play golf. If a reporter waits until after the game for, say, Madison Bumgarner, the reporter might miss Bumgarner by an hour or more. So the team makes the players available to the press as they leave the game, makes them available in the clubhouse while the game is going on. It is one of baseball's charming customs, helps explain why baseball is still the best sport to cover.

On this day, Bonds came out of the lineup early and the Giants public-relations staff said we could interview him at his locker. The media—including me—hustled to the clubhouse. Bonds was not at his locker. A public-relations man said he was taking a shower. We waited, about ten of us. It was unlikely

Bonds would say anything noteworthy, but when Bonds spoke, we had to be there. Whatever he said would be more important than the game. He was the news by virtue of being Barry Bonds.

We waited a long time. Finally, we heard the slap of his wet flip-flops on the clubhouse floor. Bonds walked toward us, world-weary, media-weary. We were bunched near his cubicle and Bonds correctly felt he didn't have enough room to approach his locker. Most people in his position would have said, "Excuse me."

An athlete bored to death with us might have said, "You're in my way." Or, "Would you move?" Or, "Get out of the way."

Anything like that would have worked—has worked a million times. Bonds didn't take that route.

He grabbed a bat as he walked forward. He held the bat by the thick end, the hitting end. As he entered the crowd of reporters, he pointed the bat straight ahead and, without uttering a word, moved us out of the way with the handle of the bat. He actually touched a few reporters. Not hard. But he touched people with the bat. He bore into us, maneuvering reporters this way and that. I wondered if it was part of my job description to be manipulated like this. He didn't hurt anyone, but he was using the bat like a tool, a cattle prod, the way a rancher would move livestock.

And his meaning was clear. We were cows or goats or pigs, four-legged, subhuman, and we didn't deserve the rudimentary politeness and consideration you would accord a human being. After getting dressed, he allowed us to interview him, an interview that amounted to nothing.

I have considered that scene so many times. Imagine if I had touched Bonds with a bat, if any media person did that. There would have been a fist-fight. Bonds would have felt outraged and assaulted, and justifiably. It would have been national news. A credential would have been revoked. The players union would have gotten involved. The commissioner, too.

Years later, my friend Barry Bloom, a national baseball writer, told me I was harsh when I wrote about Bonds. Bloom meant how I wrote about the bat incident, and how I wrote about Bonds other times. "You took what he did personally," Bloom said. "You're a professional. It's your job *not* to take it personally. Your attitude colored the way you portrayed him."

I thought about that. And it's true, I'm supposed to distance myself. But come on, Bonds treated me like a hog, prodded reporters with a bat. Damn right I took it personally.

THE ART OF DEBATE: FRANK ROBINSON BLOWS A GASKET

ONTY STICKLES AND SAN FRANCISCO GIANTS manager Frank Robinson hated each other.

Stickles, a former tight end for the 49ers, was now a sports reporter for a local radio station. He had a head like a boulder and sometimes worked as a bouncer at bars because he liked to fight, to roll on the ground and punch guys. He had been a dirty football player and was proud of it. He was well read and a good father, but his meanness came out after he drank. That's when he became a son of a bitch. And sports people—I am one of them— would say he had a hard-on for Robinson, disliked Robinson's sarcasm and tough-guy persona.

Robinson had been a great baseball player, one of the best, could be mentioned in the same paragraph as Willie Mays, Hank Aaron, Mickey Mantle, and Roberto Clemente. That great. A Hall of Famer. The only player to be named MVP in both leagues. He was the first African American manager in the big leagues, a brilliant baseball strategist, and one major hard-ass. He loved to intimidate his players, reporters, anyone. His face in yours, an almost insane leer in his eyes. Everything about him said, "I fucking dare you to cross me."

When he was player/manager for the Cleveland Indians in 1976, the big-league club played its Triple-A affiliate Toledo Mud Hens in an exhibition game. Duane Kuiper, who played for the Indians in 1976, told me this story.

Mud Hens pitcher "Bullet" Bob Reynolds had told everyone before the game that if Frank got up to hit, he was going to drill him. Apparently, Reynolds was pissed the Indians had sent him down to the minors in spring training. But Robinson caught wind of Reynolds' plan. When Robinson came to the plate, Reynolds threw one behind his head. Robinson then flied out to center field. As he trotted toward the dugout he crossed paths with Reynolds, threw two punches, and knocked him out. Remember, this was a midseason exhibition game. It was supposed to be a celebration. Full house in Toledo. After he knocked out his own player, Robinson quickly got ejected from the game. Frank Robinson was that kind of hard-ass.

He was a controversial manager. Second baseman Joe Morgan, a discerning man, considered Robinson an elite manager. But Morgan was a self-motivated future Hall of Famer, confident of his enormous ability, and didn't need encouragement. Other players who required a softer touch couldn't stand Robinson. Robinson didn't comprehend the soft touch. Disdained it. He believed you had to be tough in life and baseball. He sure had to, coming from the streets of West Oakland. He admired people like him.

I sat with one of the Giants in 1984—Robinson would get fired later that season—and this player pointed at his teammates taking batting practice.

"You see Frank at the batting cage?" the player said.

"Yeah," I said.

"Do you usually see Frank at the cage?"

I said I never thought about it.

"Why do you think he's at the cage?" the player asked.

"I don't know."

"You want me to tell you?"

"Sure."

"Because we're losing and Frank's worried about his job and wants to show management how hard he's working."

As I say, Robinson was controversial.

One day in 1984, Monty Stickles came to Robinson's postgame news conference in Robinson's office at Candlestick Park. I was there. Stickles didn't like baseball to start with and he'd wait until the seventh inning to arrive at the park. Sometimes he had a few pops on the way over and you could smell the alcohol on his breath.

The Giants had lost the game and their 1984 season was disintegrating. Robinson had used reliever Gary Lavelle, who was coming off the disabled list with a knee injury. Lavelle got shelled. Reporter Carl Steward asked Robinson the essential question: Had Lavelle looked healthy enough to pitch?

Robinson answered. Of course Lavelle was healthy. His tone was grumpy, offended. He muttered *goddamn* when he finished speaking.

Now Stickles entered the drama. Wanting to challenge Robinson, he said, "I think it's a reasonable question."

"It's a horseshit question," Robinson shouted. He almost levitated in his chair. He did not like reporters questioning his moves. Stickles started to say something but Robinson interrupted him, gave Stickles the death stare. Stickles stared back.

In the clubhouse, the players heard Robinson shout. His voice echoed off the walls of his office, a small, cramped, crowded room. Carl Steward, who had asked the original question, told himself, *If these two guys go at it, we all could die in here.*

"I'm fucking telling you," Robinson yelled at Stickles. "If he ain't fucking healthy he wouldn't be out there."

"You had to test him, right," Stickles said. Sarcastic.

"Test my ass," Robinson shot back. "It's a horseshit fucking question. I answered the fucking question. You gonna come back and ask me a-fucking-gain."

"Pardon me, Frank." Sarcastic.

"Pardon my fucking ass."

"Fuck your ass," Stickles said.

"Yeah, you wanna fuck my ass?" Robinson shouted. "You wanna fuck me?"

"Not physically, figuratively speaking," Stickles said. Stating his position.

"I'll tell you what," Robinson said. "You take that and stick it up your ass and get the fuck outa here. Get outa my fucking face."

"My pleasure."

"You're goddamn right and don't fucking come back."

"Fuck you," Stickles yelled.

"Same to fucking you," Robinson shrieked. And then he uttered the crucial words. "You fucking bum."

The air went out of Stickles. His shoulders slumped. His face looked sad.

"I'm not a bum," he told Frank Robinson. His tone defeated, almost a whine.

Robinson, who could be brilliant in his cruelty, had typed in the card catalog of his mind the weak spot of every media person he knew and would attack the weak spots when necessary. Ditto for his players. And now he had delivered the coup de grâce to Stickles because, secretly, Stickles felt and feared that he really was a bum. And Robinson knew it and had exposed him publicly and loved doing it. Stickles had no reply.

"You get the fuck outa here," Robinson shouted, seizing the advantage, dismissing Stickles who slouched off defeated, crushed, humiliated, done for.

Robinson turned to the reporters, all of us silent, ashen-faced, and with a self-satisfied smile, he said in the most reasonable voice, "Next question."

Frank Robinson, a more complicated man than I'll ever understand, did all that because he didn't like a simple question about Gary Lavelle.

06

KAEPERNICK MEETS KIERKEGAARD: WHY COLIN KAEPERNICK IS SUSPECT

S IMPLE QUESTION FOR COLIN KAEPERNICK, a mere two-word sentence: Why then?

He had been a mixed-race person all his life facing things a mixed-race person faces and, all of a sudden, six years into his NFL career it dawned on him that there are monstrous injustices in the American system. Or as he proclaimed when he refused to stand for the national anthem before games: "I am not going to stand up to show pride in a flag for a country that oppresses black people and people of color. To me, this is bigger than football and it would be selfish on my part to look the other way."

Those are fine and worthy sentiments. People of color have a rough time in America, but why this epiphany in the 2016 preseason when Kaepernick was twenty-eight years old as opposed to, say, a year earlier, or two years earlier, or anytime in his NFL career, which began in 2011? Or in college. He attended the University of Nevada, Reno, which has a predominantly white student body. He didn't feel out of place there, saw no injustice?

Or how about the Super Bowl in February 2013? He was the starting quarter-back for the 49ers, had a worldwide audience at his disposal day after day during Super Bowl Week. But he never uttered a word about injustice then, apparently had no concept of it.

So why did he refuse to stand for the national anthem in 2016? This question is the crux of the Colin Kaepernick issue. And the answer may be discouraging for people who see Kaepernick as a civil-rights spokesman, a man of deeply held principles, a hero.

He dissed the anthem because he wanted attention. Strictly my interpretation. I freely admit that.

He had been used to attention in his 49ers career. He took over for Alex Smith in 2012, Smith sidelined with a concussion, and in his first NFL start, Kaepernick threw two touchdown passes, his longest completion a phenomenal 57-yarder. After that, Smith was history in San Francisco and Kaepernick was the star. Kaepernick fell in love with himself. After throwing a touchdown pass, he would kiss his right bicep, kiss it on camera.

In May 2015, he posted on Twitter and Instagram a photo of cars underwater along with this message: *I warned you the #7torms Coming !!! #Houston.*

Kaepernick's number was 7 and Kaepernick's message had something to do with Seven Storms coming to Houston, meaning he was coming, meaning, I guess, he had caused the flood. But the submerged cars were no joke, were the result of serious storms in Houston resulting in eleven inches of rain overnight and deaths. Houston was where the 49ers would open the preseason. His posts were unbelievably insensitive and careless and full of self-love, and people in Houston were outraged. He later apologized.

He needed the glory and attention, but in preseason 2016 Kaepernick's star had faded. He was no longer the 49ers starting quarterback. He was a mere backup quarterback to Blaine Gabbert. Blaine who? Kaepernick was not one of thirty-two starting quarterbacks in the National Football League. He was just a guy. What a massive comedown. And every synapse in his brain must have fired the message: "This is wrong." It was then that he developed a social conscience and refused to stand for "The Star-Spangled Banner."

A man who had been in the news but no longer was in the news made himself the biggest news in sports. Made himself bigger than his team, bigger than the entire NFL. It was an egomaniac's dream, although, in fairness, another interpretation is possible—that Kaepernick's social awareness evolved. Certainly the causes he espoused were important and resonated in America. Still do. He focused our attention on them. I support players kneeling for the national anthem. The players who kneel do it quietly, respectfully, and with dignity, do it from the heart. But I have a problem with Kaepernick.

Disclaimer: My view of Kaepernick may be skewed because I know him and don't like him. Please factor that in. It's also possible—likely—he has matured from the self-centered juvenile I covered. Certainly, he's a complicated person.

Kaepernick advocates have compared him to Muhammad Ali as a man of moral stature. Because of his stand against the Vietnam War, Ali was banned from boxing for three and a half years, the best years of his career—what would have been the best years. But Kaepernick already was a second banana, although he regained his starting job in Game 6 after Gabbert had gone 1-4. In the final eleven games Kaepernick's record was 1-10.

People who never had met him said he was a great humanitarian and political visionary. Some media who covered him thought he was a jerk. I sure did. The worst thing about Kaepernick before he became a spokesman for the besieged and downtrodden was the constant moving.

He always spoke to the 49ers media on Wednesday, the day he chose for his mandatory weekly press briefing. Before the 49ers built Levi's Stadium with its large locker room and auditorium, they had set up a tent near the practice field for media briefings. The old locker room was small and crowded with players and equipment. To ease the tension their quarterbacks—think Alex Smith—addressed the media in the tent which had a stage and microphone. Not Kaepernick. He insisted on meeting the throng of eager reporters from newspapers, radio, TV, and blogs in the locker room.

That was inconvenient for the media, squeezed into a small space. It was also inconvenient for the players, having a media mob thrust into their midst. Kaepernick easily could have avoided all this by going to the tent. He didn't want to. He chose to make things even more inconvenient, and this is where the constant moving came in.

He would stand in front of some player's locker, not his own—a breach of protocol and courtesy in a locker room. He would wait for the media to get ready, including camerapeople who needed to set their cameras on tripods and get focused, and then Kaepernick would decide that wasn't exactly the right place and he'd move. He would zig and zag his way through the locker room, pretending to stop at a place and then he'd duck and dive and move again. He was playing a nasty game, toying with the media, making them think, "Where will he stop?" He was like someone playing musical chairs. It was so unfair because between camerapeople it's competitive, even contentious to get a good spot, not to get blocked out. They had to scramble to be in front and this amused Kaepernick. He wore a look of contempt which seemed to say, "Look at those fucking animals."

And he did all this just to do it. Just because he could do it. It was a way of exerting power, of asserting his ego, and it showed an immature lack of respect for adults, a need to prove he was in charge. He made the media trail after him like submissive dogs, forced the camerapeople to set up all over again and, of course, he'd stand in front of another teammate's locker along with the horde of tired, grumpy, sweating reporters and camerapeople. One former 49er told me, "If Colin did that to me, I'd tell him, 'Use your own goddamn locker.'"

It always amazes me that some people—Kaepernick—can be decent to groups of people in general, people they haven't met—the *oppressed*. But crummy to real people right in front of them—journalists, camerapeople.

In the 2015 season, one player had said off the record that Kaepernick lived on an island, said players on the offense rarely sat with him at lunch. They felt he made everything about himself. A quarterback is supposed to praise his teammates. A quarterback thanks his offensive line for protecting him. Not something Kaepernick routinely did. And some players couldn't get over Kaepernick asking for a trade before the 2016 season, wondered why they should embrace him as their leader, a quarterback who didn't want to be on the team.

And then came 2016. After the first game, a 28–0 win over the Rams, Blaine Gabbert was the 49ers quarterback, but there was Kaepernick holding forth to the media in the locker room on the sad state of America. One teammate reportedly walked by and said, "We just played a football game." Meaning Kaepernick had chosen the wrong topic and the wrong place.

Another player who had a good game complained to a friend no one in the media talked to him. It was all about Kaepernick. This player did not dispute Kaepernick's message but questioned his timing. The media surrounded Kaepernick, who had not even played. For team unity, Kaepernick should have deflected the focus from himself. No chance.

Kaepernick had forced his teammates into a corner. They had to say the socially acceptable thing to the media, had to say they supported Kaepernick. Privately, some felt otherwise.

No one had expected this extreme egocentrism from Kaepernick. The day the 49ers drafted him in 2011, he drove to the team's headquarters with his white adoptive parents from their home in Turlock, California. He had a warm, innocent smile and his parents were so proud of their son, who grew up middle-class and took AP classes at Pitman High School.

Looking at Kaepernick and his mother and father on Draft Day, you thought *this is a lovely family tableau*. But he never again was that lovely young man. In group interviews, he answered questions with dead-mackerel eyes, answered in the fewest possible words, each word filled with anger and condescension. He was like a man being interrogated for a crime, stingy and unforthcoming and begrudging and unsmiling. When reporters would request his insights on an opponent in the week leading up to the game, Kaepernick usually said, "They play hard. They're well coached." This all-purpose, lazy answer was a clear indication of Kaepernick's disdain for the media and his unwillingness to be frank, helpful, or polite.

Reporters counted the words of his cumulative answers in an interview session and often discovered their questions contained more words than his answers. The word disparity between questions and answers became a joke among the media. When reporters published the numbers, the 49ers public-relations staff sometimes would object, trying to protect the misanthrope.

One theory about Kaepernick implicated former head coach Jim Harbaugh. This may have been true. Harbaugh could be impatient with the media, with what he considered silly or uninformed questions and, according to this line of reasoning, Kaepernick learned from him. Perhaps, but Harbaugh could also be expansive. He is bright and plays with words and has an innocent smile that takes over his face. Few in the media saw these charming traits in Kaepernick.

And we saw a quarterback who failed to develop his playing skills, who didn't work hard at what really matters in his job—throwing the ball and reading defenses. Who declined as time went on. He was a fastball thrower even when a play called for touch and finesse. If his first receiver wasn't open, he often would not follow his progressions, look for his second and third receivers as Joe Montana painstakingly learned to do. Kaepernick would give up on the play and run—something Steve Young did until Bill Walsh told him to knock it off. An NFL quarterback wins by passing.

Week 2 of the 2014 season, the first game ever at Levi's Stadium, the 49ers played the Chicago Bears and trailed 28–20 late in the fourth quarter. On the last play of the game, the 49ers had the ball on the Bears' 17-yard line with a chance to tie the score. On fourth-and-9, Kaepernick threw an incomplete pass to Michael Crabtree and the 49ers lost. After the game, Kaepernick explained to the media what he saw on that final play. "They had Cover 3," Kaepernick said, naming the Bears defensive alignment. "We got the look we wanted. We just have to make that play."

It was a fine analysis except for one thing. He was dead wrong. The Bears were playing Cover 1. A quarterback who can't tell the difference between coverages doesn't do his homework, isn't serious.

Here is your football primer on coverages—skip this paragraph if it seems arcane. Cover 3 is a zone coverage. In zone coverage, defenders are responsible for specific areas of the field, not for specific receivers. Cover 3 features one free safety and two cornerbacks playing deep zones and four different defenders playing underneath zones—closer to the line of scrimmage. Cover 1 is man-to-man coverage with one free safety playing deep—being the center fielder—and everyone else chasing individual receivers around the field. If the Bears were playing Cover 3 zone coverage, Crabtree would have been the correct read, but the Bears were playing Cover 1 man coverage and Crabtree got smothered by cornerback Tim Jennings who was guarding him. On the other side of the field, 49ers receiver Anquan Boldin beat the man-to-man coverage and, as he ran free into the end zone, waved his hand at Kaepernick to indicate he was open. But Kaepernick didn't see him because he misread the defense and wasn't even looking that way. Kaepernick threw to the wrong man. Okay, a quarterback can misread the coverage in the tumult of the game. But not understanding his mistake a half hour later is more than routine forgetfulness. It is a quarterback not attending to craft.

When he refused to stand for the anthem starting in the 2016 preseason, fans and the media went nuts, some for him, some against him. I wrote a column critical of him, and I was wrong. After that, I learned. We all learned.

That doesn't change the basic fact. He wanted the attention. He loved the attention. After games, mostly losses, Kaepernick would talk about the state of the country in the solemn, quiet, depressed losing locker room. He would gladly explain why he didn't vote in the 2016 presidential elections or even local elections, although African Americans have given their lives for the right to vote. "I think it would be hypocritical of me *to* vote," Kaepernick lectured reporters. "I'd said from the beginning I was against oppression, I was against a system of oppression. I'm not going to show support for that system. And, to me, the oppressor isn't going to allow you to vote your way out of your oppression."

His refusal to vote had real-life consequences. Proposition 62 proposed to end the death penalty in California. If Kaepernick had done rudimentary research, he would have learned African Americans on death row far outnumber the percentage of blacks in America. The proposition failed. And Kaepernick failed too, failed to put his vote where his mouth is.

Head coach Chip Kelly, who never had control of the locker room, allowed Kaepernick to highjack the focus away from the team. Kaepernick had been a verbal minimalist but now he wouldn't shut up. At the very least, Kelly should have told Kaepernick to take his postgame show out of the locker room, a football locker room, and talk to media about the failures of America in the hallway. Never happened. Kaepernick took over the 49ers organization.

He compromised his position when he showed up one day wearing socks depicting police as pigs, a rip-off from the 1960s—think *pigs of the power structure*. This offended police, as it should have.

He compromised his position even more before the 49ers played the Miami Dolphins in Miami on November 27, 2016. It is customary for the opposing quarterback to speak to the local media—in this case Miami media—on a conference call a few days before the game. Miami sports writers couldn't help grilling Kaepernick, who now wore his hair in a 1960s retro version of a natural, his hair high and wide like a halo, and who sometimes wore a Malcolm X black hat with a white X like he was Malcolm X reborn.

It bothered Miami writers that Kaepernick had worn a T-shirt in a prior news conference featuring the faces of Malcolm X and Fidel Castro and the caption: "Like minds think alike," implying Kaepernick respected them both.

The Miami writers asked why he would wear a Castro shirt—remember this was Miami media representing a sizable anti-Castro Cuban population. Kaepernick said it wasn't a Castro T-shirt. It was a Malcolm X T-shirt. Ducking the question.

The *Miami Herald*'s Armando Salguero, born in Cuba, pointed out that someone like Kaepernick, who was protesting oppression in the United States, should understand Castro too was an oppressor, had eliminated all dissent, freedom of the press, and jailed political opponents. Kaepernick said Castro's policies led to 100 percent literacy in Cuba. Forget that Cubans routinely jumped into small boats and hazarded shark-infested waters to flee the "humanitarian" Castro. The sheer nerve of Kaepernick lecturing Cuban exiles about Castro.

Salguero wrote a column about his interaction with Kaepernick that ended with this: "So wear your Malcolm X shirt that features Castro, Colin Kaepernick. Wear it around town where hundreds of thousands of Cuban exiles live. Wear it on the field Sunday during pregame if you're so proud of it. Show everyone what an unrepentant hypocrite you are."

This story had a fascinating denouement. During training camp 2017, Dolphins starting quarterback Ryan Tannehill got injured and the Dolphins were desperate to sign another quarterback fast. Would they sign Kaepernick? No, they would not. They signed Jay Cutler, who had retired from football to become a television analyst, brought him right out of the booth. Kaepernick supporters were outraged. They said the Dolphins should have signed Kaepernick instead of Cutler, owed it to Kaepernick. Really? After what Kaepernick said in praise of Castro? After he wore the Castro T-shirt? Can you imagine the uproar if the Dolphins brought him to Miami, made him the face of their franchise?

Before the 2017 season, Kaepernick said he would opt out of his 49ers contract to test the free-agent market, although he still had time to decide not to opt out. The 49ers had brought in a new general manager, John Lynch, and new head coach, Kyle Shanahan. Lynch encouraged Kaepernick to opt out. Lynch told Kaepernick if he did not opt out, the 49ers would cut him. So Kaepernick declared for free agency but no one wanted him. He was free-falling through space with nowhere to land.

Suddenly, he became a cause célèbre with civil-rights groups, and the media latched onto the phenomenon. But most media people who took up Kaepernick's cause never had met him. They believed he was being wronged, singled out for espousing a cause and for expressing his First Amendment rights by kneeling during the anthem and speaking about injustice. It was a reasonable conclusion to draw. But Kaepernick's case did not refer to the First Amendment. It's worth looking at the wording of the First Amendment:

"Congress shall make no law respecting an establishment of religion, or prohibiting the free exercise thereof; or abridging the freedom of speech, or of the press; or the right of the people peaceably to assemble, and to petition the government for a redress of grievances."

That means the government cannot imprison you for your speech. But no one imprisoned Kaepernick. No one abridged his First Amendment rights. He said everything he wanted to say. But the First Amendment has nothing to do with one's right to employment, does not address the status of an employee who exercises his or her First Amendment rights. An employer can fire you for exercising freedom of expression, especially in the workplace, as Kaepernick did. Happens all the time. Just imagine if you start protesting at your job. You stand by your desk and tell everyone America is unjust. A crowd of workers forms around you as you declaim. You would get fired or suspended or reprimanded. Imagine if I had done that at my newspaper, took over the newsroom, wore socks portraying cops as pigs. I would be fired.

Many said Kaepernick was an elite quarterback who got a raw deal because of his beliefs. He may have gotten a raw deal but he was hardly elite. Look at the mundane facts. In 2016, Kaepernick's 59.2 percent pass-completion percentage ranked twenty-sixth of thirty eligible quarterbacks, putting him in the bottom sixth. Sam Bradford, the leader, completed 70.6 percent of his passes.

The league was not impressed with Kaepernick. That includes Arizona Cardinals head coach Bruce Arians. On September 27, 2015, the 49ers had traveled to Arizona to play the division-rival Cardinals—San Francisco got walloped 47–7. Kaepernick threw four interceptions, two were pick-sixes, the defender intercepting the pass and taking the ball directly into the end zone for a touchdown. Like the Cardinals were in the 49ers' offensive huddle. Kaepernick threw his two pick-sixes in the first six minutes of the game, an astonishing accomplishment. So, the Cardinals owned Kaepernick.

Here's what Arians said about Kaepernick before the 2017 season: "He can play in the right system. He's proven that. When he was with [49ers offensive coordinator] Greg Roman, that system fit him perfectly. He's a good read-option, athletic guy. He can throw it down the field with the play-action passes. He struggled against us in the past out of the pocket. It's just finding the right fit."

According to Arians, Kaepernick is not a good pocket passer—it's like saying a pitcher can't find the strike zone. Kaepernick needs a team that uses the read-option, meaning on a given play Kaepernick can hand the ball off or keep it and run himself. But only five teams featured that offense during training camp 2017: Seattle Seahawks, Carolina Panthers, Dallas Cowboys, Tennessee Titans, Buffalo Bills. Those teams all had starting quarterbacks, had no need for Kaepernick who reportedly wanted an opportunity to compete for a starting job. If the Seahawks signed him—they thought about it—he would have competed with Russell Wilson. There would have been a Wilson camp among the players and a Kaepernick camp. No team needed that chaos.

But let's say Kaepernick got blackballed in some form because, really, what happened to him is peculiar, all those jobs and he couldn't get one of them.

His 49ers teammates respected him. After the 2016 season, they gave him the Len Eshmont Award, the team's most prestigious annual honor for the 49er who best exemplifies the "inspirational and courageous play" of Len Eshmont, a player from the original 1946 49ers team. The players did this, I believe, because they admired Kaepernick's courage in standing up to power.

But he had offended wealthy team owners, some of them America-first conservatives who were appalled by his protest. From an owner's point of view, bringing Kaepernick to his or her team could be a disaster. What kind of teammate would he be? Would he make the narrative about himself? Would he be a positive influence in the locker room? Would he attract a media circus? Would he suggest football is irrelevant?

Owners, who invested fortunes in their teams, must have been scared stiff about alienating their fans with a quarterback who, from some fans' point of view, didn't respect America. Kaepernick should have anticipated this. What else did he expect? Coaches must have been horrified at having a protesting quarterback talking about America's sins when everyone else on the team was talking football. All reasons not to bring this headache to their teams.

Owners had their worst Kaepernick fears confirmed when the Baltimore Ravens considered signing Kaepernick for the 2017 preseason. The team's coach and general manager were interested in him, but owner Steve Bisciotti wasn't so sure. He was an owner, after all, and wondered what signing Kaepernick would do to his team and fan base. His worst fears came true when Kaepernick's girlfriend tweeted a photo comparing Bisciotti to a slaveholder. Way to go, Team Kaepernick. According to former Ravens linebacker Ray Lewis, the Ravens didn't sign Kaepernick because of the tweet. The other thirty-one owners must have seen what happened and gasped.

Kaepernick eventually reached a settlement with the NFL in which, according to reports, he split $10 million with defensive back Eric Reid, who also said the league colluded against him. The settlement is much less than originally reported.

Still, you may sense something heroic about Kaepernick, something almost biblical. He went ahead with his protests knowing he would offend powerful people and possibly doom his career.

The philosopher Søren Kierkegaard saw similar heroism in Abraham when Abraham followed God's command to sacrifice his son, Isaac. Kierkegaard called Abraham a "knight of faith." Abraham had no guarantee God's angel would stop his knife-wielding hand at the last instant, Isaac lying there about to get his throat slit, God substituting a ram for Isaac. Imagine the relief Abraham felt and the love he pledged God when the Lord spared his son.

Kaepernick had no guarantee an angel would stay the owners' hands and spare him. And no angel appeared. Risks can fail, and Kaepernick's failed—that's why risks are risky and why they matter and can define the meaning of a person's life. The risk itself is the honorable act, bravely facing the danger. Kaepernick was honorable in the enormous chance he took.

Except for one thing. Abraham had a son to lose. Kaepernick, who'd already lost his starting job, had nothing to lose.

A hero? You make the call.

NATIONAL ANTHEM: HOW THEY CHEAPEN "THE STAR-SPANGLED BANNER"

A MERICA IS OBSESSED WITH A QUESTION: Should athletes stand for the national anthem before games?

It's an important question, but it's the wrong question, the decidedly wrong question.

The correct question: Why do teams insist on playing the anthem before games?

In our society—I don't know why—sports are about patriotism. Before games, they play "The Star-Spangled Banner" and sometimes unfurl American flags the size of football fields and have flyovers from big loud armed-forces jets, the entire stadium shaking from the roar. Fans stand with hands over hearts and sing the lyrics—well, some do. In the baseball season, the anthem ritual—obligation?—happens 162 times for every team, not to mention spring training games. An absolute orgy of *O say can you see.*

Forget that professional sports and even major college sports are big business, have nothing to do with patriotism. But it pays for teams to appear patriotic, appeals to some of the fan base, not all. Makes the teams look good.

You go to a movie, they don't make you stand for "The Star-Spangled Banner." Ditto for a Broadway play. The whole idea seems silly. Yet there we are at games showing we love America. Being forced to show we love America. I love America but don't love pressure to prove it again and again in the most superficial way.

They didn't regularly play the anthem at games until World War II. We were fighting Hitler, for God's sake. Fighting for our lives. You bet people stood, and the tradition continues. The anthem wasn't even the anthem until 1931 when President Herbert Hoover signed a bill anointing "The Star-Spangled Banner." Before that we didn't even have a national anthem.

I spent my adult life standing for the anthem in press boxes. I have stood for thousands of anthem renditions, grumpily. I was not being unpatriotic. I was bored. I heard the song so many times I didn't hear it anymore. For all I knew, someone could have been singing "When the moon hits your eye like a big pizza pie." The anthem became background noise. Sounds without meaning.

Sometimes the anthem is a press-box joke. So many bad singers out there who can't reach the high notes of *and the rockets' red glare*. Laughter in the press box. Suppressed snorts. Or singers forget the lyrics. Remember Robert Goulet mangling the song before Ali-Liston II, the poor guy singing *O say can you see, by the dawn's early night*. Cue the press-box laugh track. Or singers trying to make an artistic statement, dragging out the song forever like Roseanne Barr. You'd think Beverly Sills or Pavarotti were singing arias at the Met. Amid suppressed giggles, some press-box wise guy pulls out a stopwatch and times the performance. *She's gone over two minutes!*

After 9/11, they started playing "America the Beautiful" during the seventh-inning stretch at baseball games. At first I stood for it. This was just after the Twin Towers fell. I felt emotional. I wanted to stand, and I love "America the Beautiful." After a few years, I stopped standing. That song isn't the national anthem. It's just a song—a very nice song, but just a song. I was writing my column by the seventh inning and didn't want the interruption. And I objected to publicly displaying my love for America a second time when I already showed it with the anthem.

Please stop with the anthem at games. Stop the phony, enforced association between multibillion-dollar, money-making corporations and true patriotism. Play the anthem at selected games on Memorial Day, July 4th, and September 11th, maybe Christmas Day, maybe New Year's Day. People will listen and sing with love in their hearts. And the song will have the meaning and majesty and the respect it deserves.

THE NAKED COACH: JACK ELWAY TAKES IT ALL OFF

THIS COLUMN LIVES IN INFAMY. Jack Elway was the football coach at San Jose State, had a brilliant mind for offense and, of course, was John Elway's father. I attended a football game, San Jose State playing California at Cal's glorious Memorial Stadium in Strawberry Canyon in Berkeley. I watched the game in the stands with my wife and afterward walked to the locker room to find a column topic. I bumped into *Oakland Tribune* writer Annette John-Hall outside the San Jose locker room.

"Anything going on in there?" I asked.

"Nothing, unless you consider a naked coach something going on," Annette said. A naked coach?

I hurried into the Spartans locker room and, sure enough, there stood Elway, buck naked. He had emerged from the shower and water dripped from his body forming a pool at his feet. He was all there in the all-there and he was conducting a postgame presser, writers huddled around him. I don't remember what he said,

I was too flabbergasted to take in the words. *A naked coach?*

After a while, I drifted back to the stands, which were empty except for my wife reading a mountainous nineteenth-century English novel for a class she was taking at San Francisco State, where she was in the Masters program in creative writing—short fiction.

"You get a topic?" she asked.

"Nah, nothing special was happening."

She eyeballed me.

"Something special always happens. Think."

"Well, there was the naked coach."

"A naked coach, are you kidding me?" she said. "How can you possibly pass that one up?"

"Write about a naked coach?" I said.

"Sure—his nakedness was a hostile move. He was trying to put off the writers."

I said I could see her point.

"And use your descriptive abilities." She came down hard on this. "You're a writer. Describe what he looked like."

I've always found my wife persuasive and, because she was a writer herself, she insisted on specific detail, the bedrock of good writing. I obliged her. I wrote a detailed column describing Elway's body, his protruding tummy, his chubby thighs. I did not write an X-rated column, but I wrote enough that Elway felt, well, exposed.

When the column appeared, all hell broke loose. Readers said I had gone too far. Elway, who had a wonderful sense of humor, went on TV and said now he understood why his wife turned off the lights when they made love. But he wasn't pleased. He phoned me at the *Chronicle*—I'll never forget this—and said, "I demand accountability."

Accountability? What might that involve? Were we talking swords or dueling pistols at dawn? Whatever it meant, I said I would give it to him, so I drove to his office in San Jose where he sat at his desk and glared at me. Pissed. Really pissed.

"Why did you write that about me?" he demanded.

Oh shit, I thought. *What in the hell could I say?* The truth was I had been desperate for something to write, so now I said something equally lame: "Because my wife told me to."

The room went eerily quiet. He stared at me. And then Jack Elway laughed a lusty laugh. My answer was so ridiculous he loved it.

"I certainly can understand wanting to please your wife," he said. "Let's go get a drink."

And we did.

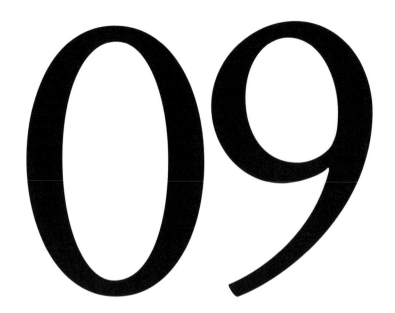

NAKED MEN:
WHY NAKED MEN IN THE
LOCKER ROOM AREN'T SEXY

NUDITY IN PROFESSIONAL SPORTS LOCKER ROOMS is not sexy. I'm talking men's locker rooms in baseball, football, basketball, and hockey—the locker rooms I covered. Places where men take off clothes and put on clothes and are naked in the intermediate stage—or are naked more than that—places where men and women reporters are present. Anyone who thinks this is sexy doesn't understand the protocol of sports, doesn't understand how scrupulous reporters are to avoid embarrassing athletes.

The athletes turn away from the room, face their lockers and quickly take off a towel and step into their underpants, then into their slacks. When athletes are doing this, the writers, if they are professionals—the overwhelming majority are—look away. Look at the wall or the ceiling or the floor. Anywhere but at the athlete, vulnerable and exposed. I certainly wouldn't want an athlete to see me nude.

Fans think I was lucky to be in locker rooms, a perk they long for. The locker rooms smell of socks and jocks. There are exposed penises. The rooms are noisy. Dozens of people mill about and you hear showers in the background and sometimes you hear music through the loudspeakers—if the team won. Silence if it lost. And athletes can be rude. Writers are there to ask questions and get answers. Not to sneak a peek.

I have watched women reporters to see if they watch. In the Bay Area never. Ann Killion, Susan Slusser, Janie McCauley, and others don't look, can't be bothered. These are grown women in serious working mode. Above reproach. No secret agenda. And I admire them because it sucks to be a woman in a men's locker room. Just sucks. For what it's worth, it sucks for a man.

I don't like having to finesse not looking at naked men, figuring out when the coast is clear—when the athlete thinks the coast is clear. This was never part of my job description when I applied to be a sports writer, although it most certainly became part of it—as integral as knowing the infield fly rule or the difference between a cornerback and free safety.

I first understood the problem in the 1980s—and it most definitely was a problem—when women, more and more, became part of newspaper sports departments. Essential additions to our business, and they were entitled to equal access in the locker room, couldn't do their jobs without it. The Giants had played a midweek day game at Candlestick Park and a woman journalist was in the postgame clubhouse. This was still new. Unusual. A Giants player, stepping into the locker room from the shower, became agitated. A player I admire for his deep-down character. A good person. Someone I keep in touch with.

He screamed at her to get out. He was wrong, of course. His issue wasn't with her. It was with the team that had issued her a credential. It was with Major League Baseball, which allowed women into the room. And it was with the federal courts, which decided in 1978 that women had equal access to men's postgame locker-room interviews. She had a right to be there, needed to be there to do her job. When she did not leave, the player yelled again. His eyes bulged with outrage.

Although history was against him, although mores were changing, and have changed, he also was right. Every bit as right as she was. This was his locker room, a place where he had undressed thousands of times without feeling mortified. In his worldview—he was a devout Christian—it was wrong for a woman reporter to see him without clothes. It was more than wrong. It was immoral. An offense to his wife and children. A denial of his values. I felt sorry for him and I felt sorry for the woman reporter.

Shit situation.

Ballplayers sometimes acted brutally in the early days. There were horror stories.

In 1990, the *Boston Herald's* Lisa Olson, whom I know, was interviewing players in the New England Patriots locker room after a weekday practice. Some players walked by her naked and made off-color comments. Some made off-color gestures. Zeke Mowatt grabbed his genitals. One naked player standing near Olson said, "Here's what you want. Do you want to take a bite out of this?" Other players joked about what was happening—all in Olson's presence.

Olson complained to the Patriots, but the team did nothing. Owner Victor Kiam made fun of her at a banquet. Referencing Patriot missiles in the Gulf War, he said, "What do the Iraqis have in common with Lisa Olson? They've both seen Patriot missiles up close." Kiam later apologized.

The NFL ordered an investigation and concluded that Olson was "degraded and humiliated" and fined the team and the offending players.

Patriots fans slashed her tires. She received hate mail and death threats. Her apartment was burglarized. She moved to Sydney, Australia, and worked for a local newspaper to get away from it all. She sued the Patriots, Kiam, and three players and finally settled the suit—the terms were not disclosed. She returned to the United States in 1998.

Here's another horror story. A well-known Bay Area athlete beckoned a woman to approach his locker. They were alone. Grinning, he showed her the nude centerfold from a men's magazine. He should have worn a sign: Sexual Harasser. Flasher. Or just plain Moron.

There were dozens of stories like those.

One time a Giants player offended me. He offended every writer waiting to interview him. He was a pitcher. Had lost an important game. Took his time in the shower. His business, but inconsiderate. It was a night game and writers were sweating deadline. He finally approached his cubicle. All the writers turned away as he reached his locker. This included the women. We were giving him every courtesy as he dressed.

From over my shoulder I heard him say—shout, actually—"Do you all want to look at my ass?"

Either he was accusing us of being interested in his sorry ass, or he was saying *screw you* in a convoluted way. I don't know what he meant. But I knew he was out of line, was rude, was what my Brooklyn friends in the 1950s would call a punk.

I know why he did it. He'd lost. Failed the team. Felt like crap. So, he took it out on us. We couldn't defend ourselves. Couldn't say, "Just a minute, sir, you've got no call to say that."

Interviewing nude players or semi-dressed (or semi-undressed) players is weird. I can't overstate its unnaturalness. When Michael Tilson Thomas, conductor of the San Francisco Symphony, finished a night's work, no reporters rushed to his dressing room, and while he was in his briefs, asked why he screwed up Beethoven's *Fifth*. It's an absurd notion—not to mention an absurd visual.

But this is exactly what happens in sports. Guys there in the altogether, or almost altogether, and someone asks, "What pitch did you throw when So-and-So jacked the walkoff grand slam?"

The WNBA, the women's professional basketball league, addresses nudity in a sensible and sensitive way. In the hubbub immediately after the game, the women sit at their lockers in their uniforms and answer questions. This media period, mandatory for players, lasts about twenty-five minutes. The media comes in, asks questions, gets answers, leaves. This system eliminates the awkwardness of naked-men's locker rooms, and because it requires players to be present at their lockers, it lets journalists do business quickly, efficiently, and unobtrusively. After the interview period, WNBA players shower and change.

WNBA locker rooms are open before games, as well—same as the NBA. During a designated period, the women wear their uniforms and are available to reporters. Male writers, not feeling the crush of postgame deadlines, often request a player from the team's public-relations person, making it clear the interview can take place in the locker room or on the court—the player's choice. Totally civilized.

Major League Baseball and the other major men's sports should adopt the WNBA model. Of course they should. Don't belittle the press by parading naked in front of them.

But male athletes, especially baseball players oversaturated with media from 162 games of exposure (double meaning there), wouldn't go for it. They make so much money now, live in a different reality from you and me. Requiring them to "behave," to appear promptly at their lockers directly after games fully dressed, no nakedness allowed—not nobody, not nohow—would be a joke, beneath them. Unenforceable.

Of course, there's a simple solution to the whole nakedness thing. Writers should be required to undress before entering the locker room. Shoes and socks optional.

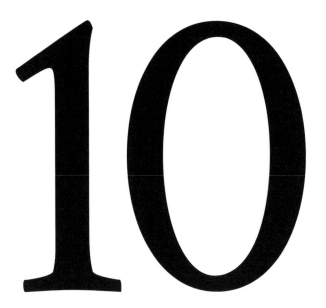

REGGIE JACKSON
DOES HIS BUSINESS

W HEN REGGIE JACKSON RETURNED to the A's for one season—1987, the final season of his career—he addressed me by name, was polite, solicitous, "How are you today, Lowell?" Once he invited me to his Oakland Hills home, where he played catch with two friends in the backyard and told me his intimates call him Jack.

But in 1982 he didn't know me from jack, as it were. He was playing for the California Angels and I was covering some of their home games in Anaheim for the *San Francisco Chronicle*. After one game, the media gathered around his locker, the usual deal because he was, well, Reggie Jackson. When the group dispersed, I lingered. I had one more question and it is common practice for a writer to ask privately if he may ask an additional question.

So, I did just that. Jackson eyeballed me. Realized I wasn't a local writer for him, was not in the LA group. I was unimportant in his universe. That, of course, is my interpretation.

"I can't talk," he explained. "I have to take a shit."

And he walked away, presumably toward the toilets.

I have wondered about that conversation for decades. Was Jackson discussing his bowel movements pure and simple? If so, God love him for being direct and elemental. Or was there something else involved? I have entertained the possibility he was indirectly calling me a piece of shit and saying someone of my low stature was not worth his time.

Language can be so complicated.

AN OLD KNEE: DUANE KUIPER OFFERS TO KICK ME YOU-KNOW-WHERE

THE SAN FRANCISCO GIANTS got Duane Kuiper in 1982 to play second base. I had read he had a bad knee, figured it would hurt his range at second. I wrote the Giants were crazy to sign a guy with an eighty-year-old knee.

Now, it was early in the season and I was in the Giants clubhouse at Candlestick Park before a game. Kuiper walked over and politely introduced himself. Said he had read my article about his knee.

"I'll tell you what," he said in the velvet voice he now brings to his Giants play-by-play announcing. He was grinning. "There's an old man outside the clubhouse right now. He is eighty years old. Let's go out there and we'll ask him to kick you in the nuts. After he's done, I'll kick you in the same place. Then you'll see if I have an eighty-year-old knee."

I said a demonstration wouldn't be necessary. I said he'd made his point. From time to time, he reminds me of that day, always with a friendly grin, always with the velvet voice. He still offers to kick me in that special place. I always decline.

MYTH-BREAKING:
BILLY MARTIN
OFFENDS THE JEWS

I HATED THE SPORTS MYTHS. Learned to hate them.

That some player was a good guy, a moral paragon, because he could hit home runs or throw touchdown passes. Pure bullshit. Fans love these myths and sports writers—some of them—perpetuate the lies.

The biggest myth-fraud I ever encountered was Billy Martin, portrayed in popular culture as a brawler (supposedly a good thing) with a heart of gold. If you only got to know him, you'd see the truth. He was the Robin Hood of the big leagues.

Really?

Billy Martin was a good second baseman on New York Yankees championship teams in the 1950s and he became a manager and won lots of games. He was a drunk. He hated women. He got into fights, for sure, but he was a sucker-puncher. He was known for that, waited until a guy turned his head and then would blast him. He had famous fights with Dave Boswell and Ed Whitson. These were men who played for him. He was smart and crafty and managed the Yankees five different times and won a World Series with them. He could motivate players before they got sick of him. One of Billy's pitchers told me he'd had enough of Billy. If Billy said anything nasty to him, he'd "squeeze his head like a pimple."

I knew Billy when he managed the Oakland A's from 1980 to 1982. He grew up in Berkeley, and the team and media made a big deal of his "homecoming." My friend, *Oakland Tribune* columnist Ralph Wiley, named Billy's balls-out style of play Billyball, a great name. And Billy's A's won the American League West title in 1981 before the Yankees eliminated them in the League Championship Series. The A's fired Billy in 1982 because of his miserable personality, because he couldn't get along with anybody, because, like a child, after one game, he took a bat and destroyed his office walls and the plumbing in his bathroom at the Oakland Coliseum when he and the A's had a disagreement. The A's had everything patched up overnight so the players wouldn't see what a lunatic their manager was. As if they didn't know.

None of this mattered to me. Not personally. It was stuff I wrote about. But there was one thing, one time that made me hate Billy. I had written something he didn't like. I don't remember what it was. I don't believe it was memorable.

Maybe Billy had a legitimate grievance. In a case like that, the manager— any manager—calls the writer into his office, shuts the door, and lets the offending writer have it. It's all part of the job for manager and writer, and it's fair—even necessary—for an aggrieved manager or player or team executive or owner to have his say, get things off his chest, even the scales. The writer listens politely with an open mind, acknowledges what the person has said, and then, the air cleared, they both move on with business and life. Things like this happened to me many times in baseball with Tony La Russa, Roger Craig, and Frank Robinson, and in football with Bill Walsh, George Seifert, Steve Mariucci, and Mike Nolan. It was a healthy self-cleansing mechanism.

But Billy never said a word to me and I didn't know a problem existed between us until I bumped into a writer from another paper. "It was disgusting what Billy said about you," he told me. He was waiting for a reaction. I didn't react. I said I knew nothing about it. And I really didn't.

The writer was surprised, thought I'd heard. He recently had been in Billy's office with another writer—someone from my paper—and Billy told them he was pissed at me. And then Billy said, "It's too bad he wasn't killed with the other six million."

That's what Billy Martin said about me and the Holocaust Jews.

Then I reacted. I phoned the second writer who confirmed what Billy said. This is important. In journalism we need two sources to confirm a fact like this. And now I had my two sources. And I had Billy by his Billyballs.

It was then that I made my mistake. I should have gone to the A's management, a Jewish management run by Walter Haas Jr., the Levi Strauss heir. I should have told him about Billy, told him I had two sources and let Haas deal with his anti-Semitic manager. This was not a sports issue. It was more important than that. But I was a young man and that mature course of action never crossed my mind.

Years later, I was faced with a similar situation and I did better. The San Francisco 49ers had signed an Australian player named Jarryd Hayne who tweeted in Australia the Jews murdered Jesus Christ. Rabbis in Australia asked Hayne to retract but he didn't. His personal manager said he was unavailable for comment.

I wrote a private email to Jed York, CEO of the 49ers, alerting him to Hayne's words. I asked York to tell Hayne to cease and desist. And I asked one other thing. Would the 49ers issue a statement disassociating themselves from Hayne's statement? I was giving York an opportunity to respond. I told York I would not write a column about Hayne at that time. I allowed for the possibility I would in the future. I never did. So I had gone through a back channel to York.

What did York do?

He told his public-relations guy to answer me in an email, to say the 49ers had contacted Hayne and Hayne would remove his tweets. Good. But the 49ers never issued a statement about Hayne, and York never got back to me, never acknowledged how serious this was, never thanked me for giving him a heads-up gentleman to gentleman and for not going public. For York, I believe, this did not rise to the level of moral issue. It was strictly a public-relations nuisance. If a 49ers player made equally incendiary comments about gays or African Americans, you can bet Jed York would have knocked himself out to clear things up. Publicly. As he should have.

York, who never has given the slightest indication of anti-Semitism, missed an opportunity to do the right thing.

Hayne eventually retracted his statements—on Twitter, of course. When he showed up for training camp and reporters asked about his anti-Semitic tweets, he said he already had addressed them. True in a sense.

I should have acted like that with Billy, gone through a back channel to the owner, but I was young and didn't have the poise. Instead I wrote a column I still like, a compare-and-contrast essay about Manager One and Manager Two, the kind of essay we wrote in high school English classes, and it ran September 3, 1982. I never used names in the column but anyone reading it understood Manager One and Manager Two managed the big-league baseball clubs in the Bay Area. It was obvious that Manager One was Billy and the other was Frank Robinson of the Giants.

I made several one-to-one comparisons:

"Manager One ran out on his team in the middle of a doubleheader. Manager Two stayed in the dugout, even when things were awful."

"Manager One got into a snit and threw over a food table in the clubhouse so his struggling team would have nothing to eat after a tough doubleheader. Manager Two believes in a balanced diet."

"Manager One banned bubble gum from the clubhouse because he got a wad stuck on his shoe. Manager Two has taken no stand on the bubble gum crisis."

Word got to me Billy was furious, although, after condemning me to the gas chambers, there wasn't much else he could do.

I walked into the Giants clubhouse shortly after the column ran. I saw Robinson leave his office and walk fast toward me. He looked serious, all business. He was an intimidating man, but I couldn't imagine he had a problem with my column. That was my hope. Who the hell was Billy Martin to him? Robinson was among the greatest baseball players ever. He hit 586 home runs. Martin managed 64. Robinson was in the Hall of Fame. Martin? Please.

Robinson kept walking toward me. He loomed over me. In a serious tone and in front of his team, he demanded, "Am I Manager One or Manager Two?" I told him to work it out for himself. A pause. The room dead quiet. And then Robinson laughed the loudest laugh, a laugh that filled the clubhouse. To me, that laugh meant *fuck Billy Martin*.

Which pretty much expressed my feelings.

13

BILLY MARTIN
SETS ME STRAIGHT

WHEN I WAS A YOUNG MAN, I wrote baseball players were not the brightest, a column I regret. But it led to one of Billy Martin's greatest moments. When he saw me after that column appeared, I thought he'd punch me. But he didn't punch me. He rose to a moment of great dignity. In a news conference in his office he said the apostles didn't go to college, and he didn't see what education or brains had to do with being a good person. I felt put down and I deserved to feel put down and I respected Billy for what he said. And when I still experience moments of distaste for him, I remember his remark about the apostles and I give him a nod.

14

A FINE HOW-D'YE-DO:
REGGIE SMITH SAYS
THE F-WORD

I DIDN'T KNOW THE MANNERS OF BASEBALL, didn't know the protocol. That's how I got in trouble with Dodgers outfielder Reggie Smith.

I was in Los Angeles covering a Giants-Dodgers series, the first time I ever wrote about away baseball, and I wanted to interview Smith because he was a good player and I heard he was talkative. This was early in the 1980 season, my first year covering baseball as a columnist, as anything.

But I was shy to approach him. My fault. I was bashful then, and I had spent years in universities where people were excessively polite, where you needed an introduction to meet someone famous. After a night game, I asked Steve Brener, the Dodgers head of media relations, if he'd introduce me to Smith. No problem. Brener took me to the home clubhouse in Dodger Stadium, a place I'd never been. We walked to Smith's locker. He was there doing nothing.

Brener started to approach Smith, then hesitated. Smith was a scary guy.

"Reggie," Brener said. Almost a whisper.

Smith looked at him. Sonny Liston stare. Said nothing.

Brener introduced me.

Smith said nothing. He got up, turned his back to us, stared at the back wall of his cubicle. I felt anger radiating from his body.

Brener kept trying. "Lowell Cohn would like to write a profile of you."

"Not interested," Smith said.

"What?" Brener said.

"Not interested."

"Why?" Brener asked.

"Can't he approach me himself?"

So I said, "I'd like to write about you. I thought it would be more polite to be introduced. I didn't want to intrude on your privacy."

Smith never looked at me. Said to Brener as though I weren't there, "Tell him to go fuck himself."

"What?" Brener said incredulously.

"I said he can go fuck himself."

And then Reggie Smith walked away.

Needless to say, I didn't get the interview. A few minutes later, Brener approached me in the press box, asked if I had a history with Smith. I said, "What history?" I'd only just started as a columnist. I'd never met the guy, never written a word about him. No time for a history.

Brener said he spoke to Smith after I left. Brener was embarrassed. Smith declined the interview, Brener said, because last year the "Bay Area press burned him pretty bad." Brener asked if I understood. I said I did, although I had only recently become part of the Bay Area press.

I sat in the press box, thought about what had happened. And the possibilities were fascinating. Maybe Smith was having a bad day. Or maybe he was pissed because his eleven-game hitting streak had ended that night? Or maybe he routinely told writers to go fuck themselves. Or maybe Smith was offended I didn't approach him myself, thought I had violated baseball etiquette, thought I was a punk for using an ambassador. And he was right. I was a punk.

But none of that is the clincher. I realized Smith did something brilliant, something I can't forget. He never spoke to me. Never even looked at me. He told me to fuck myself through Brener. I wasn't worth a direct address or a look eye to eye. I was only worth an indirect message delivered to me as if I hadn't been there. It was the best putdown any athlete ever laid on me. And I would have fucked myself if I'd only known how.

15

THE SALS: HOW SPORTS WRITING IS A FISTFIGHT ON THE PLAYGROUND

T HIS IS HOW I LEARNED to be a journalist.

Big Sal and Little Sal routinely kicked my ass when we were kids in the public playground on Avenue L and East 18th Street in Brooklyn in the 1950s. Kicking my ass meant they got me in a headlock and I gave up and then we went back to playing stickball or punchball or handball or slapball.

I never backed down from the Sals even when I knew an ass-kicking was coming. And I always got my ass kicked, but I fought back and they liked me for it. When tough kids from other neighborhoods came around and picked on me, the Sals kicked their asses.

The important things for me were standing my ground and taking what I got. No one ever taught me these skills—this courage—when I was an undergraduate at Lafayette College or a graduate student at Stanford. There is no class in ass-kicking and how essential that concept is to a journalist. To life in general.

Sports journalism is a conflict enterprise involving intimidation. You have to stand your ground against athletes and other journalists. Sports journalism is as competitive as the games we cover. Maybe other forms of journalism are like that, too.

I think of what happened when Kevin Mitchell came to the San Francisco Giants in 1987. We didn't know him, but we knew his reputation. Came from a San Diego ghetto. A tough guy who hung around tough guys. Might have been a gang member. Might use his fists. The unspoken warning was, *Don't piss off Kevin Mitchell.*

I wrote something he didn't like. During batting practice, I saw him talking to outfielder Jeffrey Leonard near second base. Leonard was another tough guy affectionately known as Penitentiary Face. Leonard was pointing at me. I imagine Mitchell asked Leonard to show him Lowell Cohn, and Leonard did just that. Mitchell walked over, said something aggressive. I don't remember what. Must have been about not getting on his bad side. The usual athlete-to-writer shit. I stared into his eyes. I'm five foot seven but I told him to knock it off. I told him he didn't scare me. Remember, I had stood up to Big Sal and Little Sal, and Mitchell had nothing on them. Plus, if he hit me, I'd own his house and cars. He knew that. Amazed, he walked away in a huff. Leonard had observed it all. He ran over to me.

"You love this shit, you really do."

"You're right, I love this shit."

Leonard smiled with appreciation. And I realized that being with big-league ballplayers was just like being on the playground with the Sals, only this was a different playground.

After that, Mitchell and I got along great. Beneath the tough-guy surface, he's whimsical and kind. I loved covering him. But I had to be strong, stake out my turf. If not, Mitchell would have despised me with good reason—just a punk sports writer, a wimp he could boss around.

Athletes understand terrorizing people. It's part of their universe. An athlete has an argument with a writer and the writer doesn't pee his pants, refuses to be intimidated, well, now they can do business. I learned these things on the Avenue L playground when I didn't know I was learning them.

I once interviewed Henry Bibby, basketball coach at University of Southern California after the Trojans beat Stanford in the Pacific-10 basketball tournament. This was March 7, 2002, in Los Angeles. Part of a group interview. The LA writers asked questions and Bibby answered minimally. Dismissive. Contemptuous. Downright rude. And the writers accepted it, wrote his crummy answers in their notebooks.

I had no questions for Bibby. I was just there listening. But now I wanted to ask a question just to ask it, to confront him. Do it for all sports writers. To balance the scales. I asked why the USC guards dominated the Stanford guards. Bibby gave a lazy answer, said he didn't know why.

"I expect you do," I said. I didn't merely say it. I shouted it. Bibby and I in the playground, everyone else looking on. Bibby blinked, locked his eyes on mine, and narrowed them to little pinpoints. Then, to everyone's amazement, gave the most detailed, generous answer. When the news conference ended, the LA writers, joyful, relieved, thanked me. They didn't need to thank me. They should have thanked the Sals. Conflict often leads to a bond between the contending parties in sports. It is a form of communication. A way to compare horsepower. Athletes and coaches admire people who face up to them.

And they understand the concept of the agenda, as in *just whose agenda are we on here?*

Athletes and coaches and team owners want things on their agenda, expect it. They expect writers to promote the athletes' and coaches' interests and their narratives. Writers have to assert their agendas if they want to get near the truth. What we have is contending agendas. Writers who cannot assert their agenda in an interview get only half the story, or no story at all. Lose before they set word to computer screen.

And here's how it works. Take the NFL as an example.

Every NFL coach conducts a day-after-game news conference, usually on Monday following the Sunday game. The coach comes in with a memorized script he's gone over with his public-relations person. What questions to expect. How to answer them. The coach does not want to be diverted from this script because, for one thing, it involves thinking. Coaches don't want to work hard for the media. And they are afraid of revealing game-plan secrets opposing coaches can use against them, even though coaches have copious film on every team they play. You'd imagine you were at a Pentagon press conference with how careful the coaches are, as if national defense depends on how they talk about their use of the safety blitz or the read-option, obfuscating the whole time.

Coaches are prepared for the first question from a writer. I ask my first question and watch how comfortably they answer, mostly in the bullshit mode. "We have to play tougher." "No one works harder than our guys, I promise you." Stuff like that.

I would insist on asking a second question, a follow-up to the first, insist even though other journalists want to speak. This is a competition and I want to win. We are basketball players going up for a rebound. I need the rebound. So, I keep talking over everyone and get my follow-up. The second question is the key. It takes the coach away from clichés and requires him to think on the spot. Sometimes, a form of truth emerges.

It could be as simple as asking a coach to define a word he had used. Coaches are not prepared to examine words. To think about language. They are used to reporters accepting their words.

When Jack Del Rio coached the Raiders, he'd sometimes say his players didn't tackle well. I'd ask what he meant by tackling well. Did the players have poor technique? If so, did his coaches fail them? Or were his players sloppy? Each question put Del Rio on the spot because, after all, he was in charge of tackling and everything else. The questions made him think, invited serious answers, and put him on the defensive—on my agenda.

And my questions carried a warning. When I said, "What do you mean by that?" it meant, "I'm listening to every word you say." It meant, "You need to be careful. This is a No-Bullshit Zone."

Or I'd question a coach's basic assumption. Once in a Monday press conference, 49ers coach Mike Singletary, a Hall of Fame linebacker, a known tough guy, told us he was putting together a championship outfit. He got worked up and started giving a motivational, locker-room speech. "I want winners. I want winners." I interrupted him, asked why he was doing that. We weren't his players. We were journalists. We had no stake in how his team performed.

He halted in midspeech. *Speechus interruptus.* He stared at me confused, a rent in his world.

"Who are *you*?" he asked, although he should have known.

I told him. His eyes bugged out.

"Are you going to be here next week?" he bellowed.

"I'm here every week."

"You can sit next to me," he said, pulling up a chair.

I said I'd be glad to. Was I the bad boy in the classroom?

When the news conference ended, he headed straight for me.

Oh, here we go, I thought. *Here we go.*

"Thanks, you make me better," he said.

Well, I thought. *What do you know?*

Singletary, too, liked someone who stood his ground. His love of competition was the best thing about him, what made him Mike Singletary.

After that, Singletary knocked off the motivational speeches to the media. Once after a postgame news conference, he quietly pulled up a chair next to me as the other reporters walked out of the room.

"How did I do?" he asked, his voice calm, even humble. Wanting my approval. Accepting my agenda. The world between coach and writer equalized.

And when that happened, I thought with pride and nostalgia, *Thank you, Big Sal and Little Sal, wherever you are.*

16

STEVE MARIUCCI
TAKES IT BACK

I WALKED INTO STEVE MARIUCCI'S OFFICE at 49ers headquarters in 2000 or maybe 2001, when Mariucci was the 49ers head coach. He was a handsome, affable man, cheerful, a good guy. I'd dealt with enough sourpusses lately and Mariucci would be a relief.

I had been in this office dozens of times to interview his predecessors Bill Walsh and George Seifert, men who had won Super Bowls, and now Mariucci. With me was Kevin Lynch who covered the 49ers for my paper, the *Santa Rosa Press Democrat*.

Mariucci was behind his big desk in the big office with a big wall of windows overlooking the big practice fields. A potentate's office. Lynch and I sat down across from him. I expected him to smile. People called him Mooch, an affectionate nickname, and it reflected his nature, a softhearted pal, a Saint Bernard of a man. But when he looked up, a black scowl marred his face, and he started yelling at me. Raising his voice. I had written something that pissed him off and he shouted lots of *fuck*s, unusual for him. I sat there and let him shout. Sometimes—not always—I could separate myself emotionally from the scene, observe it like an omniscient narrator. I observed myself and Mariucci and Lynch from a spot near the ceiling.

Mariucci kept going. He was a football coach, after all, and intimidation is an important part of the football business. He was bullying me and I enjoyed the theater of it like a spectator. I may have smiled. Finally, I stood up and pushed back my chair.

"This interview isn't going to work," I told Mariucci.

He continued yelling. Fuck. Fuck. Fuck.

As I started for the closed door, I glanced at Lynch's face, which had turned scarlet. He couldn't believe I was walking out on Mariucci, couldn't believe I had dismissed the coach.

I turned the doorknob and opened the office door. Over my shoulder I heard Mariucci say in the sweetest voice, "Come back, Lowell."

And I did. I walked right back into the office, walked across the thick expensive carpet, and sat down. And Mariucci gave the kindest, politest interview I'd enjoyed in quite a while.

DUSTY STORIES: DUSTY BAKER GETS IN TROUBLE SIGNING HIS NAME

T HIS IS A DUSTY BAKER STORY that begins with Frank Robinson. In 1984, the Giants, who would finish the season a dreary 66-96, were playing a midweek day game at Candlestick Park. Robinson was the manager then. As I was walking out of the clubhouse after the pregame media period ended, Robinson told me to stay. He was sitting at one of the orange picnic tables in the middle of the clubhouse, and he motioned for me to sit with him. This was unheard of, a manager telling a writer to remain during the off-limits time. Players stared at me. Pitcher Gary Lavelle asked me to leave.

"Lowell is staying," Robinson said.

A few minutes later, catcher Steve Nicosia, a stern look on his face, walked across the room with a handwritten poster and taped it to the locker of Giants first baseman Al Oliver, who was in the trainer's room. The poster was addressed to "O," a nickname for Oliver. The "O" meant Outcast and the poster told Oliver to take his act to Cleveland. Nicosia did all this in full view of the team, the coaching staff, and Robinson. Everyone stared at the sign. No one said a word, the room silent and tense.

What were Oliver's sins?

A few weeks earlier, Oliver said he wanted out. He said losing was depressing him, although it's safe to assume losing was depressing everyone else on the club too, including Baker, Robinson, and owner Bob Lurie. No one else asked to leave. But, okay, some people can't abide depression. Oliver's other reason for leaving was a mind bender. A trade, he said, "will give me the opportunity and the respect that goes along with getting three thousand hits. I've always been an everyday player. I should get the respect of any top player going for three thousand hits without having to check the lineup card every day to see if I'm playing."

When he said this, Oliver had the fourth-most at-bats on the team. How many home runs had he crushed? None. He had hit into more double plays than anyone in the National League. And he was complaining the Giants weren't good enough for him. One of the unspoken rules of baseball—there are so many—is to never complain about your personal stats when the team is failing. Never. It is beside the point and unspeakably self-centered. On a losing team, who gave a shit about Oliver's numbers?

He had offended Robinson, a Hall of Famer, a man who embodied baseball's codes. To Robinson, a real ballplayer doesn't bail on his team. That's as elemental as breathing. And Oliver wanted to bail, and that's why Robinson wanted me to witness Oliver's humiliation.

The poster remained on Oliver's locker several minutes. Finally, Baker walked over to his locker, next to Oliver's, stared at the poster, studied it, thought about it. He reached up and detached it from Oliver's cubicle without saying a word. Then he carefully placed it on the floor in front of Oliver's locker. Robinson looked at Baker but didn't say anything.

Oliver walked out of the training room. Every Giant in that clubhouse watched him approach his locker. Baker, an actor in a silent movie, pointed to the sign. Oliver stared at the poster while the team stared at him. He frowned. He grabbed the poster from the floor, folded it in half, and put it next to a garbage can.

"You can go now, Lowell," Robinson said.

Robinson wanted me to see what Nicosia did, wanted me to write a column about the ostracism of Oliver, wanted me to out Oliver in the newspaper. Which I did.

But surely Baker was more interesting than Robinson in that little drama. Baker's actions were so careful and nuanced. He would not sanction this humiliation of Oliver, a good player and perhaps a friend. So, in front of Robinson, he removed the poster from Oliver's cubicle, didn't care what Robinson or the team thought. On the other hand, he'd placed the poster in Oliver's path because he wanted Oliver to see what he had brought on himself.

I understood at that moment Baker, a player, had the same high-octane horsepower as Robinson the manager. He would direct this scene and make it right. And Baker was more sensitive than Robinson. Could put himself in Oliver's place. He was a leader, and that's why, later on, he became a manager.

The Giants traded Oliver to the Phillies a few weeks later.

*****

Before Baker became the Giants' manager, he was their batting coach. So this would have taken place in the early 1990s. I had given a bunch of baseball cards to a local graphologist—handwriting expert—to examine the players' signatures and analyze their personalities from the limited writing sample on their cards. The expert said Baker pressed firmly when he wrote, and he said other things about how Baker formed his letters. All this demonstrated, the graphologist told me, that Baker had a strong sex drive. I thought that was pretty interesting and certainly unexpected.

I wrote a column analyzing the signatures of various baseball players including Baker, and I never thought about it anymore. Until a few days later. I was in Los Angeles covering a Giants-Dodgers series, working in the pregame visitors' clubhouse when I heard a voice call my name. It was Baker. He was smiling but the smile was strained. He called me into the coaches' locker room so we could be alone.

"We get along okay, right?"

I said sure we got along okay. I didn't know why he asked.

"That thing you wrote about my sex drive, you don't have anything against me, do you?"

"Have anything against you? I like you."

"Well, I was just wondering."

"Wait a minute," I said. "That wasn't my analysis of your handwriting. It was the expert's. I merely wrote what he said. And he was complimentary. I mean, what's bad about a healthy sex drive?"

This didn't cheer up Baker. He stared at me.

"There has to be something else," I said.

"Well there is," he said. "You got me in trouble."

"With whom?"

"My fiancée." He was almost whispering.

"I don't understand."

"She thinks you're saying I play around on the road."

I just started laughing. I told Baker I never heard he played around on the road, wouldn't know if he did or didn't and had no interest one way or the other.

"I know, I know," he said. "I was just checking." He wanted to end the conversation, have it done with.

"I'll tell you what," I said, "I'll write a letter to your fiancée absolving you, explaining the whole thing."

Baker started laughing too. "No," he said, "not necessary. She and I worked it out. You and I are cool."

I was glad of that. And I realized, yet again, trouble invades life from the most unexpected sources—like how a man writes his name.

18

SPACE-TIME CONTINUUM: RANDY MOSS GETS HIS FEELINGS HURT

TWO SPORTS CONCEPTS PEOPLE RARELY TALK ABOUT are space and time. They are the foundations of a sports writer's interaction with athletes.

SPACE

Early 1980s. San Francisco Giants left fielder, Jeffrey Leonard, motioned for me to approach him. He had something to tell me. He was standing at his locker before a game and he moved the pointer finger of his right hand back and forth in a come-to-me gesture. The gesture was slight, almost unnoticeable. So many professional athletes had performed that finger thing to me. Sometimes it wasn't even the finger. A mere nod of the head. A raised eyebrow. The player asked and the writer obliged.

And that's what I had always done. I had obliged. I was a supplicant and the ballplayer, whatever his name, was a dispenser of information—about his hamstring, his batting stroke, his beef with management, his beef with me. Mostly, he was the dispenser of attention, something he and all athletes parcel out stingily to various reporters on various occasions, always making the reporter feel unnaturally grateful, always making other reporters pant from jealousy.

Thirty feet, more or less, separated Leonard and me. He expected me to cross the entire thirty feet. He would cross nothing. He would wait. It was his right to wait, my duty to walk the whole way. The distance was my responsibility.

I began to walk. This was something I had done reflexively hundreds of times.

And then I stopped. A feeling of weariness took hold of me, accompanied by a subversive feeling, a radical feeling, a world-changing feeling. These were feelings I'd never felt before. I just stood there, the thirty feet gaping between us wide as the Red Sea.

Leonard stared. Maybe I hadn't understood. In his mind, he was being courteous, inviting me over. I'm sure that's what he felt. He went to the second level. He spoke.

"Come here. I want to talk to you."

I shook my head. "You want to talk to me," I said, not believing I was saying this. "You come here."

I said this, I believe, because I liked Leonard and trusted him. He was a decent guy, one of my all-time favorite athletes. I might not have dared it with anyone else.

He stared at me. Had Cohn lost his grip? He never had encountered this unwillingness before. He must have felt confused in his innocent soul. Then he sat on his chair, began to put on his baseball socks, and dropped the subject. If I wouldn't come to him, there was nothing to discuss.

He never understood what those thirty feet meant to me. They were my bondage, the sign of my inferior status, the proof I was a thing and he was a person. In this case, earth-shattering in its minor way, the thing, me, finally dared say *no*.

TIME

An athlete's time is precious. A sports writer's is dispensable. That is how athletes understand time.

This unusual sense of time surely is embedded in every athlete–sports writer interaction. The sports writer wants to interview the athlete—asks for his time. But the athlete has to practice, attend meetings, sign autographs, get treatment, relax, play games. Needs to guard his time.

The athlete often tells the writer to wait. The athlete will grant time later that day, or the next day. Whenever. Time becomes a malleable thing, something to be manipulated and grabbed—imagine the athlete and writer pulling on opposite sides of a pizza dough. And the writer does wait. Learns to wait. Waiting is a big part of the job, although they never teach you that in school. So much of journalism is sitting on your ass, worrying when it's your time. If your time ever will come.

One spring training, I asked Giants shortstop Rich Aurilia for a few minutes. Asked in a polite tone, the tone verging on imploring, the tone trying to indicate I'm an interesting person, worthy of a crumb of time. He said, sure, but he had special drills right now. Come back in an hour and a half. That meant killing time in the empty press box even though the Giants weren't playing a game. I would kill time, literally murder time. My time.

After the allotted interval, Aurilia was not at his locker. I killed more time in the clubhouse trying to pretend I wasn't killing time. Finally, he appeared. He had forgotten. He had to rush home, he said. He felt bad about the misunderstanding but if I could come to the ballpark at 8:00 A.M. the next morning, we'd get the interview done for sure. I arrived at 8:00 the next morning. No Aurilia. I killed time wandering around the clubhouse, talking to writers, talking to a few players. Aurilia showed up an hour later. I walked to his locker. He saw me. "Oh, God, I forgot," he said. "I'm so sorry. I have to get onto the field. Can we talk this afternoon?"

That meant several hours later. I told him forget it.

I liked Aurilia then. And I like him now. After he retired, we often appeared on television together and we are friendly. At no point did Aurilia act in bad faith. He honestly meant to accommodate me. But he forgot because, by the very nature of things as athletes see them, his time mattered and mine didn't.

The San Francisco Giants, especially in my final years as a columnist, were time-unfriendly to journalists. It hadn't always been that way. In the 1980s and 1990s when they played in humble, outdated Candlestick Park, a game would end, and after a ten-minute cooling-off period, we would enter the clubhouse and talk to the players who dutifully waited at their lockers. Will Clark, Jeffrey Leonard, Matt Williams, you name anyone, they were at their lockers. It was part of their job to talk to the media who were on deadline, and the players were professionals about it.

That changed when the Giants moved in 2000 from Candlestick to their palace at Third and King Streets. The clubhouse has a players-only lounge the Giants enter through a rear door. Media verboten. It's like an exclusive club for elite flyers at an airport.

When writers enter the Giants postgame clubhouse, they often don't see any players at all. They see a ghost room. Most Giants have retreated to the private lounge. Fuck the media. Players stay there as long as they want. In the meantime, reporters, having entered the clubhouse after the ten-minute cooling-off period and trying not to look foolish, talk among themselves in the deserted clubhouse.

When the players feel like it, they wander from the lounge into the clubhouse one by one, oblivious of writers' deadlines. I eventually took the stance I used in college when I would wait fifteen minutes if a full professor was late for class, and then split. I gave the Giants players fifteen minutes. Period. Several times, I waited for Angel Pagan. He would show if he had a good game, show like clockwork. If he went 0 for 4, he'd linger in the off-limits room so long you thought he escaped through a trapdoor in the ceiling. I applied the fifteen-minute rule to him many times. If he were a full professor, he would have lost tenure.

*****

My most interesting experience with time—I'd call it my most fabulous experience as well—was with the Raiders. In a Monday night game in Seattle in 2006, the Raiders got shut out. Monday night games are a bitch. They start late and writers sweat to make deadline. The writers rushed to the postgame locker rooms. I waited at the locker of Raiders quarterback Andrew Walter. He said he needed to take a quick shower and would be back fast. His tone was apologetic. He needed to apologize—he'd had a terrible game.

As we nervously waited for Walter—*please hurry up*—wide receiver Randy Moss emerged from the shower. Moss was a famous player, a great wide receiver. He wore a towel around his wet waist. His locker was not near Walter's and he had no reason to approach us. But he did. He looked at us with disgust and said, "The media, I ain't talking to the media."

I didn't need any bullshit from Moss, not then. "That's okay," I said to him, "because we don't want to talk to *you*. We're waiting for the quarterback."

Moss stared at me, outraged.

"Why do you have to get personal?" he asked.

"I'm not getting personal," I said. "I'm merely telling you we want to talk to the quarterback, not you."

"Who are you?" Moss demanded.

Something snapped in me at that moment. Fully knowing where this would lead, I said, "I'm Lowell Cohn. And who are *you*?"

Moss' brains almost shot out his ears. "I'm Moss 18!" he shouted. He pointed to his bare chest. "Moss 18! Moss 18!"

The 18 being the number on his uniform, which he wasn't wearing. The 18 being his identity—the uniform number figures in the identity of so many ballplayers; they include it in their autographs, often in their phone numbers. Moss needed to establish his identity for me.

I was about to say, "So you're Randy Moss, are you? You could have fooled me. The way you played tonight I thought you weren't here." But a Raiders operative asked me to give it up. So I did.

Moss didn't. He ran from locker to locker telling his teammates that bald-headed motherfucker, meaning me, had mortally offended him. His teammates, who now had a miserable 2-6 record, didn't seem to care about Moss' problem.

Maybe the players didn't care about Moss' complaint because he was the guy who, earlier in the season, had run a very strange pass route. The play called for him to go over the middle on what they call a square-in pattern. In this case, the middle happened to be the infield for the Oakland A's. Remember, the A's and Raiders shared the Oakland Coliseum and, until the baseball season ended, the dirt infield was right there.

When the center snapped the ball, the quarterback faked a handoff to the running back. A linebacker bit on the fake and ran toward the running back. But the running back didn't get the ball. The quarterback started to throw to Moss seventeen yards over the middle, the middle a vacant cavern left open by the poor misinformed linebacker. Just one problem. Moss was nowhere near where he should have been. He had not run across the middle. The quarterback, staring in shock, pulled down the ball. He searched the field for Moss, who was running down the right sideline on a long go-route, definitely not the play. Moss even waved his hand like a happy partygoer to say, "I'm open." The quarterback threw the ball deep but there was no chance. Too late. When Moss returned to the sideline, coaches asked why he ran the wrong pattern.

"I don't run on dirt," he informed the coaches.

Now he tells them.

But that was then, and this was now, and Moss was calling me a bald-headed motherfucker. And all this happened between Moss and me because I was panicked about time, time being the overriding concern of my life. Because I wanted Walter's time and he wasn't there. Because Moss wouldn't give his time when no one had asked for it. A time prick.

I figure, in the thirty-seven years I was a sports columnist, I lost six months of my life waiting for athletes. When I die and meet Saint Peter at the gates, I plan to say, "Send me back, I'm owed another half year."

And I expect Saint Peter to reply, "Too bad, son, you should have been an orthodontist."

THE BAD-NEWS BEARERS:
WHEN BAD NEWS
IS GOOD NEWS

T.S. Eliot, noted poet and brain, screwed up. April is *not* the cruelest month.

The guy wasn't a sports writer. The Brain worked in a bank.

February is the cruelest month for sports writers. The cruelest, hands down. Ask sports writers the worst part of their jobs. They won't say rude athletes or double-talking football coaches or crummy player access. They'll say February. It's when writers can't sleep, take to drink, want to poke nails into their eyeballs, become whimpering, simpering fools.

Why?

Because nothing happens in February. It's the dead month. The void. The NFL season is over. The NFL draft hasn't happened yet. Baseball hasn't started. The NBA is winding down its endless, meaningless regular season, and the playoffs glow in the future, a distant mirage.

I wrote four columns a week. Where would four ideas come from? In February I rarely slept through the night. Sheer anxiety. About three in the morning, my wife would flag me for excessive moaning and tell me to knock it off.

In February, a columnist learns the immutable truth about sports writing: Bad news is good news. Bad news is something to write about, the Holy Grail of a topic.

Bad news often involves a player injuring himself or someone getting traded or fired or someone breaking the law. Arrests are a writing bonanza—trust me on this. Serious bad news sends fans into mourning. This stuff gives a sports writer joy. *I've been saved!*

*****

Let me drop a name.

Ray Rice.

On February 15, 2014, most sports columnists in America were fretting about having no column topic, wondering, yet again, why they didn't go to law school or become real estate brokers or bartenders. Then news broke that Baltimore Ravens running back Ray Rice had slugged his fiancée in an elevator in Atlantic City, knocked her out and dragged her body from the elevator. Everyone watched that video in horror, felt bad for his fiancée, felt Rice was a creep.

But this I guarantee. For sports columnists, running neck and neck with those feelings of outrage and sadness was something else. Gratitude—as in, *Thank you, God, for this.* Because on a grim February day when life was bleak, on a dismal day smack in the middle of the dead month, they had been granted a topic. A hell of a topic every sports columnist would be grateful for. A gift.

Most never had thought about Rice. They knew where he played, not much else. That changed in a flash. Now Rice became the center of the sports universe. They could write about the kind of guy he was, about violence against women, and go after the NFL, which, at the time, did not take this issue seriously enough.

Columnists may have felt guilty for a moment. They got over it fast. They didn't make Rice hit his fiancée. If they had been there, they would have stopped him—or at least, tried. Columnists certainly hoped she was okay. I sure did. But this was one hell of a writing opportunity. It was a path out of the February void for at least one day.

I've had similar conflicting feelings, sadness and elation, hundreds of times.

Many of these feelings involved the San Francisco 49ers, a philanthropy that keeps on giving. Starting in 2012, 49ers players have gotten arrested twenty times. Notice I didn't write twenty 49ers players got arrested, because certain players got arrested more than once. Like linebacker Aldon Smith, a bad-news superstar.

Here is Smith's 49ers rap sheet:

January 2012: Arrested for drunk driving in Miami Beach.

September 2013: Arrested on suspicion of drunk driving and marijuana possession after crashing his pickup into a tree in San Jose. Later that day, coach Jim Harbaugh allowed him to practice with the team.

October 2013: Charged with three felony counts of illegal possession of an assault weapon after authorities investigated a house party at which he was stabbed.

April 2014: Arrested for disorderly conduct and accused of making a false bomb threat at Los Angeles International Airport after being called out of the security line for secondary screening.

August 2015: Arrested for DUI and vandalism after allegedly hitting a parked vehicle with his car. The 49ers released him the next day.

After that, Smith went to the Raiders, got into more trouble. The Raiders released him.

I always found Smith a pleasant, well-spoken man. Which had nothing to do with my writing. His arrests were useful to me. I often wondered in print why the 49ers, who bragged *we win with class*, kept Smith. I knew why. Because he was talented, and they needed him to attack quarterbacks. I went after Harbaugh for allowing Smith to practice the same day he crashed his pickup. I wrote about the false myth that morality and character matter in pro sports. When it came to Smith, the 49ers had a sliding moral scale, and Smith slid off the bottom.

I won't recite all twenty 49ers arrests. But one sticks out. In March 2014, cornerback Chris Culliver got arrested for felony hit-and-run after driving into a bicyclist—driving with a suspended license, no less. That was bad enough, but what happened next was a writing gold mine. Culliver allegedly threatened a witness with brass knuckles. *Holy freaking mackerel!* He copped a plea to two misdemeanors and got forty hours of community service and a one-game suspension. That's all he got—you can look it up.

Although no one excuses a hit-and-run, the special detail in this narrative is, of course, the brass knuckles. Who in his right mind keeps brass knuckles in his glove box? Where do you even buy them?

There was a period when several 49ers players were accused of hitting women. This was an equal-opportunity antisocial bunch. Something was always cooking with those guys. I felt terrible for the women, but these were phenomenal opportunities. I could write about domestic violence in the NFL, call out the 49ers who sometimes cut insignificant players accused of it but went easy on talented ones.

For example, police arrested Ray McDonald for roughing up his pregnant fiancée in August 2014. McDonald was another charming, well-spoken 49er, and he was a good player. The fiancée showed police her bruises, but prosecutors did not pursue the case. And the 49ers kept McDonald on the team.

Later in 2014, the San Jose Police Department named McDonald a suspect in another sexual assault. The 49ers apparently thought this was too much, even for them, and released McDonald the same day.

But the topper-offer was Reuben Foster, a 49ers first-round draft choice in 2017. Sure, there were his first two arrests—one for marijuana possession, one for hitting a woman. The pièce de résistance occurred November 24, 2018, when he allegedly clocked the same woman in the team hotel. When the news broke, the 49ers immediately released him. Which prompted Bay Area columnists to wonder: What took the 49ers so long?

The 49ers always provide.

*****

Stephen Curry is someone else who provides, although not in a violent or legal sense.

He seems like a nice guy, although I don't really know him. But he often gets hurt, and when he does, the Warriors are vulnerable. And when he gets hurt, we remember, yet again, he is small for the NBA.

He got hurt in the 2015 NBA playoffs against the Houston Rockets in the Western Conference Finals, a series I covered. The Warriors were getting murdered in Game 4 in Houston, and that would have led me to a Warriors-Get-Murdered column, not bad for a playoff game—all sorts of dramatic tension. I could have explained why they lost, projected ahead to the next game, even to the conclusion of the series. I would have inserted relevant quotes, filed my story, and gone out to a late dinner. All in a night's work, nothing special about it.

But in the second quarter, special happened.

Curry ran down the court, ran fast to block Trevor Ariza's shot. Curry jumped and Ariza ducked and somehow Curry slid across Ariza's back, did a flip, and landed hard. He lay there, a pained look on his innocent face. He held his head. The Toyota Center went silent. The lovely young man and one of the league's best was down. Maybe seriously hurt.

My first thought was, *I hope Curry is okay.* Immediately after that—and I mean immediately—I thought, *This is special. This is what I write.*

I etched the scene into my mind, Curry lying there. I translated it into words as I described Curry's fall—how for a while, he was flying—then his crash landing. I made note of the stretcher they brought out, an important visual detail, even though Curry didn't need it and finally stood and walked off the court. I ran to the visitor's locker room. I waited outside. Curry walked in. I saw his father, Dell, walk in after him. When Dell came out looking worried for his son, I asked him questions. I asked general manager Bob Myers questions. I had to. It was my job. I completely disregarded the game that was still going on.

Luckily for Curry and the Warriors, the injury wasn't serious. Curry returned to the game, but for me, the game was secondary. I wrote about the dramatic seconds when Curry flew and crashed and the basketball world stopped.

Curry got hurt again in the 2016 playoffs, injured his knee slipping on a wet spot—again in Houston. He missed almost two weeks of the playoffs and never was right, and this led to the Warriors not repeating as champions. I wrote about Curry's injury and I've written about Curry's career-long ankle problems. He's a treasure in the NBA, but he pays for being small.

I look for special every time I cover a game.

My philosophy, acquired through trial and error and my attendance at countless Passover seders, is based on the first Passover question. Instead of asking myself, *Why is this night different from all other nights?* I ask, *Why is this game different from all other games?*

What made Game 4 different was Curry, his flight and fall.

*****

I retired in January 2017. But if I were writing when Giants pitcher Madison Bumgarner fell off a dirt bike in April 2017 and seriously damaged his pitching shoulder, missed half the season, won only four games, and pretty much ruined the Giants season almost before it started, I would have told myself: *Writing opportunity!* I didn't want his career to end, but that was his problem. It never came to that. I longed for the chance to explain why he was irresponsible. To explain that he put personal pleasure—and risk—before the team's well-being. I wish I'd had that chance.

Firings always hit the spot, and writers welcome them. Firings usually involve a manager, coach, or general manager. Someone important, often the team spokesman. Fire a manager or coach and the team is in for a change of philosophy or direction, as they say, and this especially applies to football where the new coach brings in his own staff and new offensive and defensive plans.

The 49ers fired Jim Harbaugh after the 2014 season, an idiotic firing that wasn't actually a firing. Owner Jed York didn't want Harbaugh and the University of Michigan did. York allowed Harbaugh to leave even though he was under contract. Both parties called it a mutual parting, but it was a firing.

I like Harbaugh. I knew him when he coached at Stanford. And I knew him even better when he left Stanford and coached the 49ers starting in 2011. He was combative with the media and moody. Writers would ask each other, "Which Harbaugh will he be today?" One Harbaugh was talkative and fun-loving, enjoyed verbal combat. Another Harbaugh would answer the simplest questions in monosyllables, act as though writers were trying to uncover team secrets. Forget team secrets. Try secrets of national security.

Toward the end of his 49ers tenure, Harbaugh grew comfortable with us, was more approachable. Sometimes downright friendly.

I came to like Harbaugh, but his firing was material for writers. I criticized Jed York, said he didn't know football. Said if Harbaugh's personality was difficult, York still needed to work with him. Find a way. That was York's job.

I wrote many times about the foolishness of firing Harbaugh. Welcomed the topic.

*****

Some of the best writing is born from conflict and what fans call *negativity*. We care about Hamlet because he's in a pickle. We don't care about him because he's nice—anyway, he's not so nice. We care about Othello because his life is a mess and he loses everything. I'm not saying Harbaugh is Hamlet or Othello, and I'm sure not saying I'm Shakespeare. I'm saying good stories come from conflict and, yes, bad news.

Here are other bad-news topics I welcomed:

When Ronnie Lott chose to have doctors cut off part of his injured pinkie in 1986 instead of submitting to a bone graft which would have required a long recovery. An amputated pinkie? What a topic! He was back playing in three weeks.

When the San Francisco Giants fired manager Frank Robinson, a gigantic personality with a gigantic story.

When Barry Bonds was accused of using performance-enhancing drugs and how that grim saga played out.

When Mark McGwire, a good guy, admitted to taking PEDs and lying about it.

When the 49ers' great linebacker, NaVorro Bowman, got hurt and didn't play so well anymore.

When the formerly elite 49ers became a laughingstock.

When Raiders owner Al Davis held a press conference, including a now-legendary overhead projector video showing a letter Davis wrote eviscerating coach Lane Kiffin whom he'd just fired.

*****

I have something to admit. I found myself making exceptions about the benefit of writing bad news, and now you'll think I'm being inconsistent. I *am* being inconsistent. I can't say where I drew the line or why certain bad-news topics depressed me, made me almost unable to type words on screen.

When Magic Johnson was diagnosed with HIV in 1991, my editor phoned me at home, dropped the news on me, asked me to write a column for next day's paper. I said yes. Writing was my job. But as I began to write, I noticed my hands trembling. I was striking the wrong keys, producing gobbledygook. I didn't know Johnson, but this news was enormous. At the time I didn't understand much about HIV and AIDS. Many people didn't. I thought Johnson, that great player, that wonderful personality with a billion-dollar smile, was given a death sentence. So did my editor. He phoned back an hour later, said he'd been reading the wire and learned HIV did not always lead to AIDS. It hasn't led to AIDS in Johnson's case. I wrote more easily after I spoke to my editor the second time. But I didn't like writing that column. It was the saddest column I ever wrote.

I felt the same in 1999 in Arizona when Steve Young suffered a career-ending concussion in a Monday Night game against the Cardinals. Cardinals cornerback Aeneas Williams sacked Young when 49ers running back Lawrence Phillips missed a block, sacked him hard. I was at that game. I like Young. Maybe better than any athlete I've covered. He is a warm, generous man and, unlike most athletes, was interested in the writers who covered him. After the game, he didn't seem addled. In the column I wrote from that game, I wrote he was *lucid*. His words made sense, but I thought he was in danger. He'd suffered so many concussions in his career, seemed oblivious of the danger.

"What if you get knocked out next week, or the week after?" I asked.

"We'll have to deal with it," he said. "We'll deal with them as they come. I feel like I'll know. You know what I mean?"

I didn't know what he meant. He didn't either.

I should have written my column telling him to retire. Just get out while he had a functioning brain. But I didn't. That was the last game Steve Young ever played. Thank God.

Why these exceptions? I'm not really sure. Maybe getting too close to my subject. Get close, and you lose perspective. As a journalist, I tried to avoid that. As a person, well, it's inevitable.

*****

Sometimes—many times—the great sports columnist Red Smith was stuck for a topic, like the rest of us who confront deadlines. We were on a flight from New York to Los Angeles during the 1981 Yankees-Dodgers World Series, flying through the night on the writers' charter. Red was old, frail, but he still flew after a night game, would arrive in LA with no sleep and go to the team workouts. We got to talking. Smith, a gracious man, seemed interested in me. I was thrilled to be in his presence. We spoke about the Series, two guys who scribbled for a living talking ball. Then, looking for guidance, I worked up the nerve. "What happens when you have no topic?" I asked.

Red smiled a knowing smile. He had been there so many times. "I tell myself, 'The Lord provides,'" he said.

The Lord does provide. Sometimes in unlikely ways. Ask any sports columnist. Ask in February.

HARD-ON FOR JOSEPH CONRAD: WHY I FLOPPED AT *SPORTS ILLUSTRATED*

T HIS IS ABOUT THROWING UP FROM HAPPINESS. But that comes later. It all started with a tuna-fish sandwich and a blue tie.

I was in my late twenties and I felt—believed—it was time to make a leap in my sports writing career. Not that I had much of a career for leaping. It was the mid-1970s and I was living in Palo Alto near the Stanford campus. I had published a few articles locally. I went out to lunch with legendary *New York Times* sports writer Leonard Koppett who lived in Palo Alto, and he told me to phone *Sports Illustrated* and ask for a job. Just like that. I said I was scared. He laughed at me.

So, one day I picked up the phone and dialed *Sports Illustrated* in New York. It was an experience of fear and trembling. The receptionist came on the phone and I asked to speak to the editor-in-chief.

And she connected me.

As I heard the phone ring, I swallowed hard, and when the man answered I blurted out, speaking faster than normal people speak, "This is Lowell Cohn. I'm calling to inquire about a job." All in about a second and a half.

The editor did not die laughing. I could hear him chewing. It was lunchtime in New York and his chewing sounded wet, the kind of wet you get when your lips smack into a tuna on rye heavy on the mayo. He said he wasn't the one to call, his voice tuna-liquid. I was about to get the heave-ho and I knew it, but he said, "You want to speak to Jeremiah Tax and he's right here."

Jeremiah Tax, a senior editor, took the phone. Asked about my background. Patient. Said I lacked experience—"but if you're ever in New York, drop by. I'd like to meet you." I told him I'd be in New York in three weeks to spend Christmas vacation with my parents. "Send me some writing samples," he said.

*****

A week before the flight to New York, I drove to the Stanford Shopping Center and bought a blue tie at Macy's. I wanted to make a good impression on Jeremiah Tax. The tie was soft thick wool and it was a deep dark blue and it went with my blue blazer, my one dress-up jacket.

I phoned Jeremiah Tax from my parents' apartment in Brooklyn and he said, "I've been expecting your call."

He'd been expecting my call?

He asked me to come to his office the next day. Sunday. On Sunday morning as I was getting ready to leave, my father said casually, "That's a nice tie. Is it new?"

I said it was.

"How much did it cost?"

If I knew then what I know now, I would have said:

"It was a gift," or—

"I bought it at the flea market for fifty cents," or—

"I found it in the gutter."

But I was nervous about going to *Sports Illustrated* and wasn't thinking strategically. I told the truth. "Twenty dollars." A lot of money in the 1970s but not *that* much. I noticed my father's face go red with white blotches.

"Twenty dollars!" he shrieked. "No one spends twenty dollars on a tie. Certainly not you. You don't have a pot to pee in."

One of his favorite expressions.

My dad had grown up in the Depression and he valued a buck—and there was something else. Although I supported myself teaching freshman English at various junior colleges, driving from one to another in my dirt-brown Datsun he had bought me, and although I wrote film and drama reviews for the *Palo Alto Times*, I wasn't entirely able to support myself and my dad kicked in five hundred a month. To him the blue tie at twenty dollars seemed an unforgivable self-indulgence verging on moral depravity.

I wanted to explain the blue tie made me feel good, presentable, ready for the interview. But he screamed, "Eve!" My mother.

She rushed out of their bedroom fearing strangulation or heart attack. My dad held onto my tie leading me like a pony. "Eve, he has the nerve to spend twenty dollars on a tie."

My mother stared with horror at the evidence. At the cut-rate places she shopped she could have bought twenty ties for twenty bucks. "Shush," she told my father in a soothing voice. He was breathing hard. They spoke in Yiddish, something they always did when they didn't want me to understand. A whole generation of parents extinguished Yiddish in their children. The forbidden language. She was probably telling him not to blow a gasket.

"We'll have to discuss your lifestyle when you get home, young man," my father said, as if I routinely engaged in human trafficking. Then, as I wobbled toward the front door of our apartment, he said in a suddenly cheerful voice, "I know you'll impress the editor. Knock him dead."

Thanks, Dad.

I walked the few blocks to the subway. I had sweated through my shirt. I rode the Brighton Line staring out the window until it went underground at Prospect Park and after that the dark calmed me. We rattled over the Manhattan Bridge, something I had done thousands of times, the dirty East River below.

Jeremiah Tax was a chipper little man wearing a sports shirt open at the top. Right off the bat, he held up one of my stories and bought it for five hundred dollars. I hadn't even sat down and already I'd made a sale. I could refund the twenty to my dad. It was a story about playing street games like punchball in the playground across the street from our Brooklyn apartment, and about historical continuity in our neighborhood and about Homer. I'm serious. To this day I love it the most of all my articles. Jeremiah Tax repeated I was too inexperienced for a job at *SI*. He said there would be assignments for me in the book, chances to prove myself. He called the magazine the book. The word assignments sounded glorious.

I left *Sports Illustrated* and wafted down the street as I imagined my byline in *Sports Illustrated*, on that shiny paper in that gorgeous all-color magazine. This was before the Internet when *Sports Illustrated* was still the heartbeat of sports writing in America, when serious writers like George Plimpton and Dan Jenkins and Frank Deford contributed to the book.

If I had been sophisticated, I could have strolled around Manhattan, say, down to Battery Park just to blow off steam. Or bought a drink at some swank hotel bar where the bartender puts mixed nuts in front of you without asking and asks *do you want to open a tab?* But I wasn't sophisticated. I did what I knew. I grabbed a quick sandwich at a grubby luncheonette and got on the subway toward Brooklyn because I didn't have the imagination for anything else.

My heart pounded. I felt dizzy. Lightheaded. As the old train strained over the Manhattan Bridge toward Brooklyn, my lunch rose in my throat. I choked it down. I thought I would vomit right there on the train in front of everyone. I wondered why I felt like puking at this moment of triumph and I came up with an insight into human nature or maybe just my nature. It had to do with extreme excitement of the good kind or the bad kind. I realized my nerves and ganglia and neurotransmitters and whatever else is in there can't tell the difference between extreme upset and extreme happiness. They just feel the intense stimuli, and in this case, the stimuli were extremely intense. Off the chart. Stimuli are all the same to nerves. Alarms and bells and whistles. For all my nerves knew, a mugger was chasing me through the D Train.

We descended into darkness. The next stop was DeKalb Avenue. I could get the hell off there, but the train was taking its time. My mouth had a funny taste. Finally, the train pulled into the station. As the doors opened I rushed off, pushed my way through the crowd and ran to the far end of the platform. Alone. I leaned over the platform and let it rip. Gagging sounds. Chest spasms. My lunch onto the tracks. In the entire recorded history of Western civilization I probably was the first person who vomited from sheer happiness.

I wiped my mouth with a Kleenex and went to straighten the blue tie. Wet orange streaks ruined the new blue wool. The telltale sign of reverse peristalsis. Oh dear. I took off the tie. Dropped it in a trash can. Twenty bucks down the dumper. I grabbed the next train and took it to Avenue M and walked to the apartment and told my dad about the sale and Jeremiah Tax and assignments and never once did he mention the blue tie.

*****

Now I get to Gilbert Rogin, *SI*'s managing editor, the head guy. I sold several articles to *Sports Illustrated* as Jeremiah Tax watched over me like a protective angel. Mostly, the articles were short pieces recounting an adventure. I flew in a hot-air balloon and wrote that up for the magazine. Rode a motorcycle that went on water—and sank it. Rode a recumbent bicycle. Jeremiah Tax said I needed to "upgrade" my stories, write longer, more complex pieces.

I sold Jeremiah Tax on a feature about a triple jumper/painter named Milan Tiff for three thousand dollars. After it ran, I dropped by *SI* for a meeting with Julia Lamb, an editor I often worked with. Her phone rang. I heard her say my name. When she hung up, she said Gil Rogin, who recently had become managing editor, heard I was in the building and wanted to meet me. Julia walked me to Rogin's office. I expected to see Zeus sitting behind a desk, but Rogin was a Jewish New York guy like me. He stood up. Gracious. Said he liked my writing. I sat down. He encouraged me to write longer pieces as I'd done with the triple jumper. He wanted my work in the book. Then he asked about my background. Like a job interview. I told how I grew up in Brooklyn and went to Lafayette College in Pennsylvania. He nodded. He was taking in everything. Seemed interested. I said I went to graduate school at Stanford.

"Oh," he said. "What did you do there?"

He sat up straighter.

"I did a PhD in the English Department."

This he didn't expect.

"And when did you finish?"

"1972."

"Hmm. Whom did you write about?"

"Joseph Conrad."

Rogin lurched in his chair as if an earthquake had hit the Time-Life Building. Air rushed out of the room.

"Joseph Conrad," he said.

"Yes," I said.

"Don't write like him," he said.

That was it—don't write like him. I tried to imagine why Rogin nearly levitated when I mentioned Joseph Conrad. Maybe he thought my writing weak in comparison to that genius, a great prose stylist up there with Nabokov and Joyce. I was about to ask when Rogin stood up, said he had to run and showed me to the door.

Rogin was what you'd call a notable minor author. He published short stories in the *New Yorker*, a big deal, and he published novels. He got good reviews. Maybe he was slumming at *SI*. I don't know.

I felt my chances for getting hired at *SI* were good, even though Rogin's reaction to Joseph Conrad was strange, but in the next few weeks, the *San Francisco Chronicle* offered me a sports columnist job and I took it. This was before laptop computers, before you could write for a New York publication from California. I didn't want to live in New York. I grew up in New York. That was enough for me. I took the job at the *Chronicle* and never again thought about Gilbert Rogin until years later when I was covering a San Francisco Giants game at Candlestick Park. One of my Stanford professors, Lucio Ruotolo, walked into the press box. He was a Giants fan and got access to the press box—that was before 9/11, and security wasn't severe then. We chatted, happy to see each other. Then his face went serious.

"I need to tell you something," he said. He looked embarrassed.

An admission.

"I went to Columbia with Gil Rogin," he said. "We're friends."

Where was this going?

"You wouldn't have gotten that job at *Sports Illustrated*," Lucio said. "It's good you went to the *Chronicle*."

I stared at him.

"Gil didn't like you," Lucio said.

"I only met him for ten minutes. How could he not like me?"

"It wasn't really you he didn't like," Lucio said. "He didn't like Joseph Conrad."

"Let me get this straight," I said. "Gilbert Rogin didn't like me because he didn't like Joseph Conrad?"

"That's right," Lucio said.

"What did Rogin have against Joseph Conrad?" I asked.

"No idea," Lucio said.

Rogin had a hard-on for Joseph Conrad. Why? I still don't know. Maybe

Rogin had a trauma in high school reading *Heart of Darkness*. But, sure, it wouldn't do to use Conrad's prose in *Sports Illustrated*, to copy his style, which, of course, I was incapable of doing. Imagine these words in *SI*: "It was the stillness of an implacable force brooding over an inscrutable intention." That would hardly work for Muhammad Ali's knockout of George Foreman.

But I wasn't Joseph Conrad. I didn't write like Joseph Conrad. Rogin got that right. English was Conrad's third language after Polish and French. I wrote American prose. I had studied Conrad. That was all. I can't even read old Joe anymore. Had enough for a lifetime. Rogin's reaction was like detesting William Shirer for writing about Hitler. I've often thought about Rogin's attitude. What if I told him I wrote on Henry James, more difficult even than Conrad? Would Rogin have thrown me out of his office? Or, God forbid, I was a Faulkner guy. Rogin might have committed homicide.

Which means this story has a double first. I'm the first person who vomited from sheer happiness, certainly at the DeKalb Avenue Station, and the first person, I'm sure, possibly the only person, who didn't get a job because someone had a hard-on for Joseph Conrad.

I recently looked up Rogin on the Internet. He died in November 2017. He'd had a promising career in fiction until something happened in 1980. He submitted a short story to the *New Yorker* but Roger Angell, the fiction editor, rejected it.

I used to know Angell. He is a brilliant baseball essayist and would come to spring training in Arizona and hang at the back of the media pack when we interviewed players at their lockers, Angell looking Socratic. We had dinner together a few times, Angell and I and Chub Feeney, who had run baseball operations for the San Francisco Giants and had been president of the National League, and Bill Rigney, who had managed the Giants, Angels, and Twins and now was a special advisor to the Oakland Athletics. Rigney embodied the rich oral tradition of baseball, knew everyone, told stories with a beginning, a middle, and an end, told them with tone and style, making personalities come alive—Leo Durocher, Jackie Robinson, Billy Martin. And we all sat quietly and listened and paid homage to Rigney. Imbibing baseball. Angell had a warm laugh and he appreciated Rigney and I liked him for it.

Angell had rejected Rogin's story because, according to Rogin, Angell said he was "repeating himself."

Rogin told the *New York Observer* magazine, "That motherfucker literally demoralized me. Repeating myself? I repeated myself in all my stories. My entire life is a repetition. But Cheever repeated himself. And Roth repeated himself. Saul Bellow, after a while, essentially repeated himself. So did fucking Tolstoy!

"No one had ever said anything like that to me before. I thought it was beneath me to ask how that bonehead thought I could make the story work. His rejection was a put-down of me."

Gil Rogin = John Cheever?

Gil Rogin = Philip Roth?

Gil Rogin = Saul Bellow?

Gil Rogin = Leo Fucking Tolstoy?

Unnerved by Angell's rejection, Rogin slammed into a writer's block of heroic proportions, lasting more than thirty years. He never wrote fiction again. This because Angell rejected one story, although Rogin already had sold thirty-three stories to the *New Yorker*. A fabulous batting average. It's not like Angell rejected Rogin as a person. Just a single story. But Rogin took it personally.

I've thought maybe Rogin needed fresh material. Needed to develop his style. He might have considered writing like Joseph Conrad. Say what you want about Uncle Joe, he had a pretty successful career.

THE WINEGARDENS:
STREET GAMES IN
NEW YORK

Note: This is the first piece I sold to Jeremiah Tax at Sports Illustrated, *after which I vomited at the DeKalb Avenue subway station from sheer happiness.*

I N THE FLATBUSH SECTION OF BROOKLYN WHERE I GREW UP, the streets have numbers and letters instead of names. Facing Avenue L between East Seventeenth and East Eighteenth Streets is a playground a block wide and two blocks long. It holds only three or four trees but everyone calls it "The Park."

Until 1959, when I turned fourteen and entered Midwood High School, my life *was* The Park. I lived across Avenue L from it and could peek through my bedroom window to see what games were going on there.

If I liked what I saw, I would run out of our apartment, sprint across the street, past the corner where the Good Humor and the Bungalow Bar men competed for business, past the sign that read NO BIKE RIDING, through a pack of twenty kids on their bicycles, past the checkers players, chess players, skating rink, park house, kiddie pool, and out onto the "court."

The court, the epicenter of my life, was an oddly shaped concrete quadrangle with baselines and bases drawn on it in fading yellow paint. What could have been deprivation turned into opportunity for invention. Every irregularity in the court surface, every crack or corner or crevice became the stimulus for a new game or a new rule in one of our games. We were imaginative. Had to be. Because no two playgrounds were the same, games varied from neighborhood to neighborhood, sometimes from block to block. A home-court chauvinism sprang up, a feeling we could beat anyone at our games with our rules in our place.

But something went on more significant than the games. We had been presented with a landscape of asphalt and brick and metal. No streams, hills, woods. Sometimes no sun or blue sky. Everything lifeless, from the gray sidewalks to the streets numbered or alphabetized to the elementary schools PS 193, 199, 152. Our landscape was not something we "lived" in. It was a medium we moved across.

The games changed all that. A crack in the pavement, once incorporated into the game (as a base in tag, for instance), was no longer alien, out there, and totally unrelated to us. Every time we used one of these things, we humanized it and made it our own. We became a part of our surroundings—and they a part of us.

Nothing proved this better than punchball as we played it at the Avenue L Park. Punchball is a variation of baseball played with a hollow pink rubber ball with the same size and bounce as a tennis ball but none of the fuzz. It looks like a bald baby tennis ball. Manufactured by Spalding, everyone called it a "Spaldeen."

Play begins when the batter throws the ball up over his head and swings at it with a clenched fist. The motion closely resembles a tennis serve, including the loud *thwack* at contact. Provided he has a live ball, a good player can punch it two hundred feet. After the punch, the "batter" runs to first base, a square drawn in chalk on the concrete.

The feature that made Avenue L punchball unique was the conformation of left field. In place of a fence, the back wall of a six-story, red brick apartment house abutted The Park there. If the batter hit the wall on the fly—quite a shot—and the left fielder caught it off the wall before it hit the ground, the batter was out. But the long-ball hitter had a way around this.

The apartment house wall was not uniform. In left center, a courtyard about twenty feet by twenty feet was cut into it. None of the tenants ever used it. A fifteen-foot fence guarded the courtyard. If a batter could punch the ball over the fence and into the courtyard—or the Winegardens, as the place was called—it was a home run. Not easy. A batter had to place his hit precisely or the ball would bounce off the wall and get caught. The few kids who could punch it into the Winegardens were treated like immortals.

As soon as I started going to The Park on my own, about age seven, I joined the punchball devotees who practiced all day and felt awe for the best punchers among the big kids. When I would see someone new, my immediate question was, "Can he hit it in the Winegardens?" Nothing else mattered. And like everyone my age, I lived for the day I could do it.

It was quite a while before I learned why that courtyard was called the Winegardens. One day word spread through The Park: "Winegarden's coming tomorrow! Be here." So that was it. Before my time there had been somebody, probably named Weingarten, who had punched the Spaldeen into the courtyard so many times the spot came to bear his name. Some kids said he could hit it onto the apartment house roof.

The next day everybody was there early for Winegarden's arrival. "Do you think he'll hit it in there every time?" we asked each other. We waited and we waited, expecting Zeus or at least Hercules. He never showed. But that didn't matter then and it sure doesn't matter now. I choose to believe in Winegarden, in his existence and his prowess. How else could the courtyard have got its name?

About a year ago, I was visiting my parents in the old neighborhood. Walking through The Park on my way to the subway, I overheard one little kid say to another, "Can you hit it in the Winegardens? I'll bet I'll do it before you." Then I understood the meaning of the whole Winegarden thing. We had transformed a dirty, bottle-ridden area behind a beat-up fence, named it, elevated it, made it mythical. We created a hero we shared with everyone who ever played—or will play—punchball in the Avenue L Park.

Like Homer, we were in the oral tradition, but we didn't know it. The tale of the Winegardens got passed down by word of mouth from generation to generation. It has given our neighborhood a bond of sorts and a sense of continuity. It gratifies me.

THE TEMPLE OF BASEBALL

A SCENE IN 1981

J IM LEFEBVRE, batting coach for the San Francisco Giants, is not someone you'd accuse of being a poet. He played his entire major-league career for the Dodgers, was Rookie of the Year in 1965, once hit twenty-four home runs in a season, was part of the Dodgers all-switch-hitting infield, played five years in Japan, has a square jaw, and once decked Dodgers manager Tom Lasorda.

You expect a lot of things from Lefebvre. You just don't expect him to resort to poetry. But that's exactly what he did in the deserted dugout at Phoenix Stadium during spring training. He was a John Keats in baseball togs.

Lefebvre was telling me about the function of spring training, the usual re-dedication stuff, when all of a sudden, he was *overcome*. That's the only word for it.

"When I think of a stadium, it's like a temple," he said. "It's religious. Sometimes I'd go into Dodger Stadium just to be alone. The game might start at seven, and I'd get there at one and sit in the stands and look at the field. It was that beautiful. No one would be there—only the birds chirping. And I'd see the sky and the grass. What a feeling!

"After a while, things began to happen. The vendors would come in slowly. The place was beginning to come alive. It was like it had a heart and it was beating slowly, softly—*boom, boom.*" As he said this, Lefebvre began to pump his right hand—open, shut, open, shut—like a man preparing to give blood.

"The fans started to arrive. The lights went on. *Boom, boom.*" Open, shut, open, shut. "The visiting team arrived. You could see them in their dugout and you'd look at them. *Boom, boom.* And the game was getting closer. And the heart was beating faster." Open, shut, open, shut. "And the game started. BOOM, BOOM! It was loud now, crashing, beating wildly." He was squeezing so fast the veins popped out in his arm.

"And then it was over. Just like that. The vendors left. The visiting team was gone. The heart stopped.

"I think a baseball field must be the most beautiful thing in the world. It's so honest and precise. And we play on it. Every star gets humbled. Every mediocre player has a great moment.

"The field is beautiful in spring. I smell the grass again and remember how I loved the smell, the way it came into my nostrils and filled me up."

"Did artificial turf change that?" I asked.

"Artificial turf was a desecration," Lefebvre said. "It violated the temple."

"Which stadium is the most special?" I asked.

"Yankee Stadium," he said. "I was a Yankee fan until the day I signed with the Dodgers. I had always dreamed of playing there, but I was never in it until . . ." Lefebvre paused, did a quick calculation. "It was the World Series, just after Junior [Gilliam] died, 1978."

"What was it like when you were finally in Yankee Stadium?"

"I went there and I almost cried," Lefebvre said. "It was very moving. My God, Ruth played there, and Gehrig. They were heroes and they hit in the same box, ran the same bases. They left their spirit there. I know it."

Lefebvre paused, looked at me and blushed. He had been caught with his sensibility down.

"I hope I made myself clear," he said shyly. "I've never said those things before. I didn't know they were in me."

23

MICHAEL JORDAN
DISAPPOINTS

I T WAS MICHAEL JORDAN'S FAREWELL, the final farewell. He had left the
Chicago Bulls in 1993 briefly to be a bad minor-league baseball player.
He came back to the Bulls in March 1995, then retired in 1998. Didn't
play for three seasons, then joined the Washington Wizards in 2001. And
he was retiring again, retiring forever this time. He really was.

He was taking a victory lap through the arenas of the NBA, and on March
23, 2003, it was Oakland's turn. He was appearing in Oakland for the absolute
last time against the Golden State Warriors. A chance for Oakland to honor
his brilliant career, to honor the player and the man, a paragon of deportment.

Media from all over Northern California engorged the arena, filled press
row and the downstairs work area and the media eating room. This was a
once-in-an-epoch event. To honor the great Michael Jordan. To record his
final famous words in Oakland.

A friend of mine, Dr. Jerry Kram, asked if he could attend Jordan's farewell. I got him a credential from the Warriors. He had been a Warriors doctor and now he was a Warriors season-ticket holder, and this Jordan moment meant something to him. Jerry and I had attended college together, had been friends since the age of sixteen, and I wanted to do this for him.

During the third quarter, one of the Warriors public-relations representatives walked over to me on press row. He was worried. He said the Warriors offered Jordan their interview room for his postgame media session, the interview room with a stage for Jordan and a chair and a microphone and a bottle of chilled spring water and sufficient seating for the unusually large number of reporters. But Jordan refused the comfort of the interview room, said he would talk to the reporters in the Wizards locker room. The PR person apologized to me, apologized to all the reporters for the inconvenience.

Afterward, the media piled into the visitors' locker room, a cramped, dreary, small, gray space. Jordan stood by his locker, his back to the media. He was changing into his street clothes. I remember the eye-piercing white of his shirt. No other players were at their cubicles. No room for them. Jordan turned around, flashed his million-dollar smile at the reporters who circled his cubicle seven and eight deep, commuters on a New York subway train at rush hour pushing each other, jostling for position, holding on for dear life. I could smell body odor.

Everyone was there for Jordan. Just for Jordan. To hear what he'd say after his final game, the last time he'd ever display his skills in Oakland, his skills the essence of physical poetry. Someone asked a question and Jordan, still grinning, so handsome, answered. But almost no one heard him.

If you weren't in the front line—those five or six people—you couldn't hear. Because Jordan was whispering. Whispering on purpose. People behind me stretched out their hands bearing digital recorders and phones to pick up the slightest syllables of Michael Jordan. I got an elbow in the nose. But the recorders and phones hardly picked up the Jordan sound because Jordan kept his voice low, almost a hiss-like background noise.

He kept smiling. A winning smile. People pushed forward. I felt flesh and bone on my back. Jordan was working on his tie. Dr. Jerry Kram knew basketball players well. Had taken care of so many Warriors who treated him with respect and called him Doc. But Jerry wasn't Jordan's doctor. Jordan didn't know Jerry and accorded him no respect. Jerry cupped a hand over his ear to hear something. He frowned. I cupped a hand over my ear. Heard nothing. But I saw Jordan, such a handsome man. He would come across well in the video and still photos even if almost no one heard him.

And as I stood there, pushed and pulled and sweating, stuck in the mass of reporters and wanting to get out but unable to move, I thought about what makes a person good, what makes Jordan good. Take away all the extras—the junk, really—the sneaker deals, the fame and glamour, all those externals, all those things that are not the core of a person, not the core of Jordan. What makes a person good? Because when you die, the questions you have to answer are simple: Have I been a good person? Have I led a good life? Did I try?

And I looked at Jordan and thought so much of this man is image, packaged, made up. Sure, he may be a good person to those close to him. How would I know? But he isn't acting like a good person now. He's being mean for no reason. To exert power. To disappoint people who came to celebrate him.

Why would anyone do that?

The crowd dispersed. Jordan went on dressing. Jerry and I began to walk out of the locker room. As we reached the door, Jerry stared back into the room, stared at Jordan who was alone now, the great Michael Jordan, neat and stylish like someone who'd stepped out of *GQ*. Jerry's face was sad. Disillusioned. His worldview had undergone a tectonic shift. He learned what every sports writer learns his first week on the job. Image has nothing to do with reality. Jerry had been enamored of the Jordan he never met, the Jordan he'd seen play or act in commercials. And now he had met Michael. The real thing. The man himself. Just a man, a person like everyone else.

Jerry pointed at Jordan and, using the perfect two-syllable descriptive for someone who acted as Jordan had acted, he said to me plainly and simply, "Asshole."

THE PERMUTATIONS OF
OFF-THE-RECORD

I T TOOK TIME, but I learned the various degrees of off-the-record. A complicated concept and so crucial to building trust with sources.

The lowest level of off-the-record is *for background only*. Someone in the organization gives you the lowdown on how ownership is at war with the general manager. You salivate when you hear this, but you can't write it. It's for background. And you've agreed to that. Of course, if you can get another source to confirm this, you can write it.

The second source could be a well-placed person who confirms the war between ownership and the GM. You can't quote this person or even write this source exists, but now you have two sources and you write the column.

Or it could be two well-placed people who confirm the war. They allow you to quote them, but you can't use their names. So, you write, "two well-placed sources who requested anonymity said," etc.

Or it could be two sources who allow you to identify their positions without using their names. So, you write, "two sources in the organization who requested anonymity said," etc.

Before you start an off-the-record interview, you need to establish the level, the guidelines, and people need to believe you understand the rules and won't violate the agreement.

I learned off-the-record in every permutation. In 1987, a 49ers player told me Bill Walsh was illegally drug testing the players—at the time it violated the rules of the NFL and was illegal in San Francisco. The players were too afraid to protest. I couldn't use the player's name or say he was a player. He asked me to do my own research. I checked out what he'd told me. The player was telling the truth. I wrote a column blowing the whistle on Walsh. He went out of his skull with me, but he stopped with the drug testing.

Off-the-record conversations took place in the most exotic locations. I once left my wife in a restaurant in Bodega Bay, a beach town north of San Francisco, and talked in whispers to a Giants player on a pay phone. I met sources in out-of-the-way restaurants; in dive bars; in parked cars in dark, deserted parking lots; in the dugout hours before games.

One local manager often told me inside stuff about his team. His thoughts about the players, who was going to be traded or benched, who was in the doghouse, what he thought of the general manager, the owner. He wanted me to write it as long as I didn't mention him. I'd identify my source as someone close to the manager. Once, he went on TV and said he couldn't understand where I got my information, his voice accusatory. I had to laugh.

25

LATRELL SPREWELL'S HANDS-ON EXPERIENCE

IT WAS MONDAY NIGHT, DECEMBER 1, 1997, a Monday night like any other Monday night. Not a lot going on. I had eaten dinner and done the dishes, and now I was watching TV and drinking a glass of red wine when the phone rang about 8:00 P.M. It was a public-relations man for the Golden State Warriors.

I wasn't happy to hear his voice, thought he was promoting something and wanted me to write about it. He heard my lack of interest.

"I think you better get over here right away," he said, meaning the Warriors headquarters in downtown Oakland.

"Why?" I said.

"Because Latrell Sprewell just choked the coach."

Holy shit. What the PR guy told me was that Latrell Sprewell, the Warriors star player, had choked coach P. J. Carlesimo. You bet I got over there, just in time for the news conference. The team had set up a table on the gym floor. At the table sat Carlesimo and general manager Garry St. Jean. The media stood in front of the table and stared at St. Jean and Carlesimo, who wore a turtle-neck sweater, obviously covering up the choke marks on his neck. This was an all-timer, an experience I'd never had before: "Player Chokes Coach."

In a quiet voice—I'd say an embarrassed voice—St. Jean said there had been an altercation and Sprewell had, well, choked Carlesimo. But when we asked Carlesimo questions, he was vague and seemed annoyed we were there, annoyed he was there. Really put out.

I knew St. Jean well and, while Carlesimo ducked question after question, St. Jean would steal glances at me. He seemed to be sending me a message I took to mean, *Can you fucking believe this shit?*

There had been trouble leading up to the choking. During preseason, the Warriors conducted a workout in the Napa Valley. I had arranged to interview Sprewell after the workout, but when the team opened the gym doors to the media, I saw Sprewell hurry out an exit door. Someone told me Sprewell and Carlesimo weren't getting along, meaning Sprewell wasn't in the mood to get interviewed, to say nice things about the coach. So, sure, I knew there was tension. But, holy mackerel, nothing like this.

After the post-choking news conference broke up, someone with knowledge of the situation—the assault—filled me in. It had been a standard workout. No fights. Nothing like that. At one point, Carlesimo told Sprewell to slap a little mustard on a pass. Just that. A little mustard. Apparently mustard was a spice too far and Sprewell flipped. Threatening to kill Carlesimo, he grabbed the coach around the throat. Imagine if Carlesimo had told Sprewell to put hot sauce or, God forbid, chili pepper sauce on the pass. Sprewell might have pulled out a gun and shot him.

According to my source—not sauce—the original choke took place near the free-throw line, but it didn't end there. Locked onto Carlesimo's throat, Sprewell dragged him backwards through the key toward the basket, dragged him like a stuffed doll. This lasted about ten seconds before players and assistant coaches saved Carlesimo by prying loose the maniac's hands. My source acted out the drama for me location by location like someone demonstrating the Stations of the Cross.

Practice resumed minus Sprewell. Can you imagine practice actually resuming? But Sprewell wasn't done. He returned a few minutes later and went after Carlesimo all over again. Punched Carlesimo in the face but never got a handhold on the throat. Assistant coaches saved Carlesimo yet again.

Sprewell had history. He once fought with teammate Jerome Kersey and later returned to the gym with a two-by-four and, according to reports, said he would come back with a gun. Another time he punched teammate Byron Houston three times at practice. As they say in cop shows, Sprewell had form. The league suspended him without pay the rest of the season after he strangled Carlesimo. He never again played for the Warriors, although he lasted seven more seasons in the NBA.

Why did Sprewell find Carlesimo so irritating? It could have been Carlesimo's personality. Amend that. His personalities, plural.

Carlesimo had a delightful public personality. This was the personality he used to interview for jobs in the NBA and to charm the media. He was smart and verbal and funny. He loved opera and good food, loved talking about the history of hoops. An overall great guy. But running neck and neck alongside that personality was Carlesimo the hard-ass, Carlesimo the autocrat, Carlesimo the disciplinarian. Some players called him Police-imo. People in the Warriors organization quickly became aware of the two Carlesimos. Sprewell certainly did. Or maybe Sprewell had a mustard allergy.

The Warriors fired Carlesimo twenty-seven games into the 1999 season. His record was 6-21 at the time. In three seasons with the team he went 46-113.

This story has a coda. St. Jean, the Warriors general manager at the time, is a wine lover, what you'd call an oenophile. The *Press Democrat* asked me to arrange a wine tour with him in Sonoma County. We'd take a limo to various wineries. I'd copy down his tasting notes and write a column about St. Jean, the Robert Parker of the NBA. We had the date set. My paper had hired the limo. I was pumped. Then the choking intervened.

One night my phone rang. It was St. Jean, his tone uncomfortable.

"Could we postpone the wine tasting?" he said.

"Why?" I asked, disappointed.

"I just don't think it would be a good look—player chokes coach, general manager goes on wine-tasting spree with reporter."

Point taken. Hold that cabernet.

WHY SPORTS WRITERS
ARE "YOU GUYS"

I T WAS IN BASEBALL THAT I LEARNED to love the third person.

In my life "BB," before baseball, I was accustomed to people referring to themselves as "I." Strictly first person. Strictly boring. As in, "I need to phone you back because they're going into Final Jeopardy!"

First person was a fairly standard grammatical form, one I never thought twice about. Until I started covering major league sports. Pretty soon, I interviewed players referring to themselves in the third person. It was a life-changer.

My first exposure to third-person diction was with that great second baseman Joe Morgan when he played for the San Francisco Giants. Morgan is—or was—a third-person talker, although I can't credit him with inventing this mode of speaking. I admit, with one thing and another occupying my time, I haven't fully researched the topic. For all I know, Achilles referred to himself in the third person, said things like, "Achilles plans to kick Hector's ass," as he chased poor Hector around the walls of Troy.

But Morgan, as I recall, would say things like, "Joe Morgan has to do what's best for Joe Morgan." As if he was referring to somebody else. I would look around the room for this other Joe Morgan. But there was no other Joe Morgan. It was just Joe and me.

Pretty soon, other players began calling themselves by their names, like they were corporations: IBM. General Motors. Amazon.

"Walmart has to do what's best for Walmart."

I began to think, if third person is good enough for ballplayers, it's good enough for me. I imagined coming down for breakfast. My wife is at the stove. I say, "Lowell Cohn will have scrambled eggs with linguica this morning." I say, "Lowell Cohn wants an onion bagel lightly toasted and schmeared with cream cheese." I say, "Lowell Cohn desires cream and two sugars in his coffee and will read the sports section while he waits."

I know what my wife would say: "If Lowell Cohn wants scrambled eggs with linguica and an onion bagel lightly toasted and schmeared with cream cheese and coffee with cream and two sugars and the sports section, Lowell Cohn can bloody well get them himself."

*****

It was in sports that I became "you guys."

Before covering sports, I was Lowell. Just Lowell, a fairly unusual name. I know. In my whole life I've met two or three other Lowells. We could form a very small club called Lowells of America. My parents gave me that very New England first name so I could feel American, could be part of the prevailing social fabric. Lowell as opposed to Moishe or Boaz or Jacob.

But when I wrote sports I wasn't Lowell anymore. I was "you guys." So was every other sports writer, even the women. They were "you guys," too. We were all "you guys."

It was a form of collective address from athletes and coaches, and it was not said with respect. More like, "What kind of crowd is this I'm subjected to? What form of primitive life are these people?"

And who could blame the athletes? They are prime physical specimens and millionaires, and we are underpaid, out-of-shape scribblers, some with pear-shaped bodies, sitting there wearing the kinds of shirts where if you buy one, you get one free. One time a sports writer said he could run as fast as Jose Canseco. Canseco, who ran very fast, smiled. He challenged the sports writer to a race. "How much are we running for?" the sports writer asked. "Twenty-five," Canseco said. "Twenty-five dollars?" the sports writer said, up for the contest. "Twenty-five thousand," Canseco corrected him. The race never happened. Two separate realities.

"You guys" write in little reporter's notebooks with ballpoint-pen ink on our fingers, or record the players on our cell phones and ask them questions that really piss them off. We are the "you guys" who make athletes nervous. We may find out something unsavory about them, write that they're on the outs with ownership or, worse, tell the world that they should get traded.

It can make players hate "you guys."

So "you guys" is what they call us. We don't deserve a name. They lump us in a catchall category that makes us objects instead of subjects. And that is the eternal conflict between writers and ballplayers. Who is the object and who is the subject in the ongoing interaction? Who has the dominant point of view?

I can tell you writers never call ballplayers "you guys." We call ballplayers by name. On the other hand, my wife calls me "guy," as in, "Guy, can you take out the garbage?"

JOE MORGAN'S
CLEANING LADY

I HAD A QUESTION FOR JOE MORGAN, Hall of Fame second baseman. This was years ago, when Morgan announced baseball games for ESPN. I've long forgotten what the question was. It doesn't matter.

I valued Morgan's opinion because he was bluntly honest, had a gift for analysis, and was one of the smartest sports people I ever met. He could have been a lawyer, a professor, head of a corporation, anything he wanted.

He was on the road for a game when I phoned his hotel room. He politely told me to call back in an hour, he was in a production meeting. When I called back, I was feeling pretty good about things, pretty good about Joe Morgan and me.

"Hello," he said.

"Hi, Joe. It's Lowell."

Silence.

I thought the phone had gone dead.

Then from hundreds of miles away—it could have been thousands—I heard Morgan cough like he'd got a small fishbone stuck in his throat and was choking. Never a good way to start an interview.

"I'm not going to talk to you," Morgan announced when he'd recovered himself.

Quite a change from an hour before.

"You won't talk to me?" The tone incredulous.

"No."

I didn't expect the brush-off. Joe and I always got along great from when I'd covered him as a player. And now this.

"Okay, I understand we won't do the interview. But may I ask why?"

"I didn't like what you wrote about me."

Nothing new about this line. Heard it hundreds of times. I said, "I get that you're sore at me but, honestly, Joe, I don't remember what I wrote. I haven't written about you recently. If I wrote something unflattering, please tell me. What did I write that pissed you off?"

Another silence. A long one. Finally, he admitted he didn't know what I wrote. And then he came up with this classic.

"My cleaning lady read the column and didn't like it."

Well, let me tell you, that was an all-timer. Many athletes had been angry at me even though they hadn't read the column. "Someone told me what you wrote and I didn't like it" was a standard line that always induced contempt in me or other writers for the sheer laziness of it all. But this was a whole new level of rejection. According to Morgan, as I remember the conversation, this sagacious housekeeper not only cleaned Morgan's hillside Oakland mansion overlooking the Bay and San Francisco—I'm sure she did a bang-up job—but she was also a literary critic with enormous influence over her boss. If I understood correctly, Morgan talked to reporters, or didn't talk, based on her thumbs-up or -down while maybe she was polishing the dining-room table or swabbing out the commode.

After he hung up on me, I told myself Morgan had to hold on to this wonder woman at all costs. Whatever he paid her wasn't enough. Hell, if she was looking for work, I'd hire her.

28

RITUALS:
LOVE IS STRANGE

W E MET IN A BAR. Out-of-the-way place. He was a Bay Area head coach or manager. I won't say which.

We would talk sometimes, talk about his players, talk about management, talk about him. Talk at places no sports people went. Deep off the record like the meetings never happened.

We ordered beers. It was 7:00 P.M. and we were in no hurry. That was the key point. No hurry. We could talk for hours.

He was critiquing one of his players—we were on our second beer. Said he'd like to replace him but didn't see it happening. He sighed at the injustice of life. A young woman walked to our booth. I thought she was a waitress, seeing if we needed refills. But she wasn't a waitress.

She addressed the coach-manager by his first name, her voice insistent.

"When will you be done?" she asked.

"In a while," he said.

She walked away.

She was good-looking. I noticed that. And young. I figured twenty. Her hair was up and her lips red. I took her for a college student. Cheerleader type. She had that look.

The coach-manager and I got back to business. He was having trouble with management, didn't trust the people above him. This was his constant complaint, a constant complaint with most coaches-managers. They need players. They need to win now or they get fired. Management doesn't always cooperate. Management thinks about cash flow, takes the long view. Coaches-managers take the short view. A fundamental disagreement.

He ordered another beer. Held his alcohol well.

Cheerleader came back. Used his first name again. I told myself she wrote for the college newspaper. Pissed me off he'd scheduled an interview cutting into my time.

"When will you be done?" she asked again, an edge in her voice.

"In a while," he said, barely glancing at her.

She left. I thought she was persistent for a college writer. I had to admire that.

We kept talking. In spite of his other appointment, he didn't hurry me. Answered all my questions in detail, even got into his coaching staff. Who was an asset, who wasn't. A thorough man.

We had been together two hours, more or less, when Cheerleader returned a third time. Pout on her lips. When she said his name, her voice whined.

"When will you be done?"

"Can't you see I'm talking to Lowell Cohn," he snarled. She flinched, stricken. She had no idea who Lowell Cohn was. Nor did she care. She just stood there, didn't move.

Finally, it dawned on me. *What a dope I am.* I got up to leave.

"What's your hurry?" he asked.

She sat down at the table. He didn't look at her.

I knew his wife. I wondered if he and Cheerleader did this often. Was it their usual prelude, their ritual? Who knew? Too complicated for me.

On the drive home, I sang Mickey and Sylvia:

Love

Love is strange

Lot of people

Take it for a game

VIDA BLUE
SAVES MY BACON

JOHN "THE COUNT" MONTEFUSCO WAS SHOUTING AT ME. My fault. I had made a fatal mistake—call it a rookie mistake. In the interest of in-depth immersion reporting, I decided to ride the San Francisco Giants team bus from Manhattan to Shea Stadium in Queens in June 1980 for a game against the Mets. It was my first year on the job as a sports columnist.

No ballplayer wants a sports writer on the team bus. The Giants especially didn't want me. I had been critical of them. Nothing unusual in that. But there was something else. The Giants were populated with born-again Christians—the so-called God Squad—and, as a joke, I had written the team should sacrifice one player's soul to the devil to make the Giants a better team. I never thought twice about it after that, but now I was walking down the aisle of the bus with Montefusco shouting at me, telling me to get off, and other players shouting at me while sweat poured down my armpits. I felt a hand grab my wrist and pull me into a vacant seat.

Johnnie LeMaster. The Giants shortstop.

LeMaster was one of the God Squadders. He also was a lovely man and he felt for me, understood my fear and vulnerability.

"Sit here," he said. "You'll be all right."

The shouting died down. As my migraine kicked in, LeMaster said, "You told us go to the devil." He was mortally offended. Afraid for his soul. I said my column was satire. He didn't know from satire. I said I didn't take the devil literally. He said he did. He tried hard to understand me. I wasn't sure I understood myself.

We were talking two different languages. Two worldviews in collision. Which made his gesture, his act of kindness, even more noble because he was protecting the apostate. In all my years covering sports, I found the born-agains praiseworthy because they lived up to their ideals. Tried to. And LeMaster was the proof.

After we discussed the devil, the soul, and satire, we chatted about normal things. Two guys on a bus. He calmed me down and I never forgot what he did. I also never again rode a team bus.

When we arrived at Shea, I sat in the visitors' dugout gulping air. I wasn't ready for the Giants clubhouse. Not yet. Some Giants players were hanging around the dugout but no one noticed me until pitcher Vida Blue showed up. Blue was a phenomenon. In 1971 with the Oakland A's, he had a 24-8 record and won the Cy Young and MVP awards. A's owner Charlie Finley had wanted Blue to change his name from Vida Blue to Vida True Blue. Rumors said Finley offered Blue ten grand to make the change. Not true. Blue told Finley no dice. He was Vida Blue Junior—Blue's mother called him Junior. And changing his name would be disrespectful to his deceased dad who had worked twenty years in a steel foundry. Blue was proud of his name. He went against custom, had his first name Vida printed on the back of his A's uniform, did this long before Ichiro Suzuki put Ichiro on the back of his jersey. From his playing days, only two players called Blue "True Blue": George Brett and Amos Otis. "I give them a free pass," he once told me.

Blue had a whimsical personality, found life absurd and joyful. Manager Frank Robinson affectionately called him Blue Boy. For his walk-up song they played Gershwin's "Rhapsody in Blue." Blue didn't know about Gershwin. This was long before United Airlines used "Rhapsody in Blue" as its theme song. Blue asked why they played that particular song for him. Someone told him about "Rhapsody in Blue." He was pleased, but for walk-up music he would have preferred the Temptations.

Later that season, he came over to me before a day game at Candlestick Park. I was wearing a jacket and tie. He shoved a bat into my hands, walked me to the outfield, and stood me in front of the wall in foul territory.

"You need to experience the Vida Blue fastball," he announced. "When you're an old man, you can tell your grandkids you stood in against Vida Blue."

His fastball was called the Blue Blazer.

I held the bat, the wall at my back. Blue wound up and then I heard a loud crack behind me. It was ball hitting wall. I know it was the ball because I saw it ricochet off the wall. I never actually saw the ball leave Blue's hand or speed toward me. I went weak in the knees. And then he said, "Now, let's do it again."

But that Vida Blue fastball scene would come months after the trip to Shea Stadium. Following the harrowing bus ride, I was in the visitors' dugout in New York trying to be invisible, when Blue, whom I didn't know, walked over to me.

"Are you Lowell Cohn?" he said.

Here we go again, I thought.

"Yes, I'm Lowell Cohn." I didn't want to be Lowell Cohn.

"You're the guy who wrote we should sell one of our souls to the devil."

"Yes, I wrote that," I said, preparing for Migraine Number Two.

Blue slid his arm around my shoulder. "Well, you're okay by me," he announced. He said this in front of his teammates, dared anyone to contradict him. He was Vida Blue. His teammates stared at the dugout floor, left me alone from then on. Turns out Blue had issues with the God Squad. Oh, he liked them. It wasn't a question of animosity. But he believed—feared—the born-agains took losing as God's will and tended to accept losing. Blue did not believe losing or winning had anything to do with God and he fought like hell to win.

I'm not sure Blue was right about the God-Squadders. But that's not the point. Until that day, I believed I was covering a baseball team. I was wrong. I had wandered into the middle of a deep religious debate, one that defined the Giants at that time. I've never been sure how I stand on the existence of God, but if there is a God, He sure sent LeMaster and Blue to save me. That alone could make anyone a true believer.

*****

Now it's 2017. Vida Blue and I are on the phone, going over details of this story. I remind him that Frank Robinson called him Blue Boy.

"That's right," Blue says, "Frank called me Blue Boy."

"Did he do it because of the painting?"

Silence on the phone line.

"The painting?" Blue says. "What painting?"

"The famous painting called *Blue Boy*."

"I never heard of it," Blue says.

"You mean until I just mentioned it, you never heard of *Blue Boy*?"

"That's right."

"Do you think Frank knew about the painting and that's why he called you Blue Boy?"

Blue laughs. "Frank didn't know about any *Blue Boy*, Frank growing up on the streets of Oakland."

I hear Blue tapping on the keys of his computer.

"What are you doing?" I ask.

"I'm looking up *Blue Boy*."

Silence.

"Here it is," Vida Blue says. "Thomas Gainsborough painted it in 1770. Long time ago. And it's not *Blue Boy*. It's *The Blue Boy*."

More silence on his end. I imagine him studying the painting online, gazing at the Blue Boy's impossibly shiny blue outfit, his right hand holding a hat with a feather on it, his left hand on his hip, his look straight at the viewer one of arrogance mixed with entitlement, a little androgynous dandy.

"You know what I think," Blue finally says.

"What?" I ask.

"Truthfully, this Blue Boy, Lowell, he's not exactly a swashbuckler."

30

CHOOSING UP SIDES: JOSE CANSECO ADMIRES BO JACKSON

JOSE CANSECO HAS GOTTEN BAD PRESS. Most of it deserved. He admitted taking performance-enhancing drugs and ratted out players who took PEDs. Canseco had another side, an attractive side. He was and is smart, verbal and playful. He once called Will Clark a three-toed sloth. The image was interesting and what Canseco said got around.

This scene took place in the late 1980s. Kansas City was playing a midweek game against the A's at the Oakland Coliseum. Hours before the game, that great two-sport athlete Bo Jackson walked into the A's clubhouse. Unusual for a visiting player, a Royal, to visit the other place. None of the A's said anything. This was Bo Jackson.

He walked down the line of cubicles to the very end of the room where Mark McGwire was dressing. McGwire smiled at Jackson. They obviously liked each other. They talked a long time. Talked privately. Sometimes, they laughed.

Canseco's locker was in the same line of cubicles but way at the other end of the room. Canseco kept stealing looks at Jackson and McGwire. Would look furtively. Didn't feel comfortable walking over and joining in. Didn't seem to.

After a while, Jackson started to leave, strolled through the room in his stocking feet. Canseco watched him walk out the clubhouse door. Then Canseco turned to McGwire and the rest of his A's teammates. As if they all were teenagers choosing up sides in a schoolyard game, Canseco said in his most earnest voice, "Can we have Bo?"

31

"MY, MY, MY, LIKE THE SPIDER TO THE FLY": THE ESSENCE OF DON NELSON

D ON NELSON WAS QUITE THE GUY. I was sure of it. This was 1988 when he'd become coach of the Golden State Warriors the first time, and I did a one-on-one interview with him, felt the glow of his warm personality, the beam of his gentle eyes.

When the article came out, he phoned me, that soft voice with a chuckle that conveyed, *I'm just a hick. Be good to me.* He said he really liked the article. Said I was one of the best sports writers in America. Not that he knew much about writing, he said. Right then, I was feeling pretty good about Don Nelson and me.

"I have one question," he said.

"Sure, anything, Don."

"There was a quote in your story from an anonymous source. Who was that?"

Boing!

People had tried to weasel information about my sources, but never this frontally, this shamelessly, this balls-out blatantly.

"You know I can't reveal a source," I told Nelson.

He laughed a folksy, self-deprecating laugh—his specialty—and asked if I couldn't break a rule just this once. I told him no. I told him never ask about my sources.

So, I learned about Don Nelson from the get-go. His praise had a price, was almost certainly insincere. He had an agenda. He thought he could manipulate sports writers, and in many cases, he was dead-on right. He was not a thinking man—he was a basketball coach, nothing more—but he was a savvy, smart man, a strategist on and off the basketball court. Still is.

Another personality lived behind the gosh-oh-gee, swell guy. The hidden personality was closer to the truth. He worked hard at promoting the reality of the made-up personality. I'll call that personality "Nellie." He called it Nellie. He encouraged everyone to call him Nellie. Just a regular guy, the name somewhat feminine. Nellie, your favorite aunt who lives on a farm in rural Illinois and bakes apple pie and lets it cool on the window ledge. Aunt Nellie who remembers all the grandkids' birthdays and knits in her off-hours and is the sweetest old thing. There was nothing feminine about Don Nelson, but his Nellie persona was the kindest, least-threatening being on God's Earth.

I never called Don Nelson "Nellie." If you called him Nellie, you risked getting personal and getting enveloped in his sphere of influence. I would correct people on TV talk shows with me when they called him Nellie on air. "His name is Don Nelson," I would say.

A sports writer never calls a sports figure by his nickname. We are not on a nickname basis. Although he grew up on a farm, Don Nelson is not Nellie; Tim Lincecum is not Timmy; Pablo Sandoval is not Panda.

One time, Don Nelson walked over to press row before a game. He was holding a gold watch. He said it was an extra watch, who wanted it? One eager-to-be-noticed writer took it. Guy was owned for life—or at least, for Nelson's life with the Warriors.

But I liked Don Nelson. I really did. He had one of the biggest personalities of any sports figure. Other people with big personalities I covered: Al Davis, Frank Robinson, Steve Young, Dusty Baker, Jon Gruden, Jim Harbaugh. They were a writer's dream. Dickens could have made each the protagonist of an eight-hundred-page novel.

And there was something else about Don Nelson. Sure, he was trying to pry information from me in that conversation—someone in the Warriors organization told me he was a "user." But when he didn't get the information, he ceased and desisted. He had tested me and I had passed, stood my ground. He figured the test was worth a try, it must have worked so many times. And now he had a nondiscloser on his hands and he respected me for it. Liked me for it. At least we understood each other, and on that basis, we did business for many years. But I never trusted him.

He had learned from Red Auerbach—the best NBA coach of his generation—when he played for the Celtics. He would sit in Auerbach's office and ask him why he did this or that in a game. Auerbach took an avuncular interest in the eager young man. Nelson imbibed strategy from Auerbach, whom I spoke to one time. I was writing an article about the legendary parquet floor at the old Boston Garden and, over the phone, told Auerbach I heard there were dead spots on the old floor and the Celtics knew how to lure opponents onto them so their dribbles would come up flat and they would lose the ball. Auerbach was silent for a moment. Then his voice boomed over the phone, "The floor's the only good thing in that fucking place."

Auerbach also taught Nelson cunning, shrewdness, how to play the angles. Nelson told me Auerbach would order the custodial staff at Boston Garden to turn off the radiators in the visiting locker room on freezing winter nights. Nelson chuckled at the memory.

Nelson was a brilliant basketball coach, although he had zero interest in defense. He loved the poetics of offense and spent his time thinking of ways to score. He was one of the first to understand the importance of three-point shooting. "A three-point shot is worth 50 percent more than a two-point shot. Just think about that," he once told me. He was way ahead of the league, and the league has adapted to his thinking. It is a three-point league now.

Even before he converted to the three-pointer, he used a certain brand of basketball. He identified the weakest defender on the opposition and ran play after play against him. Don Nelson was a basketball predator. And it was interesting to watch his teams murder a defender. He liked fast ball, running ball, and, although his teams never were the best, they were thrilling.

He could be revealing in startling ways. Once, he invited me to his condo in Alameda for an inside-look-at-the-coach column. He led me through all the rooms like my mother did with dinner guests at our Brooklyn apartment. He showed me all his Warriors memorabilia, including a Warriors ottoman in the living room. He showed me every bedroom. He introduced me to his girlfriend, Joy—Miss Joy, he called her. Afterward, he and I took his dog for a walk. I had something on my mind.

"Don, when I write this article, how do I refer to Miss Joy? She's not your wife. I want to do this right."

He thought a while. "I don't know what you should call her," he said. "I lost my fortune to my first wife."

That was a frank admission and I'm not sure how it applied to the article or to Miss Joy. Finally, he said, "Call Joy anything you want."

He married Miss Joy in 1991 and they've been married ever since.

After being away a decade—he coached the Knicks and Mavericks—Nelson came back to coach the Warriors in 2006. The first time I went to his office, he said, "I thought you had died."

His relations with the media were fraught in his final four seasons in Oakland. He left a game in Madison Square Garden with eighteen seconds remaining in a Warriors loss, just up and left the bench and walked to the locker room. He had seen enough. Imagine if a player had walked out. When I asked him about it, Nelson dismissed me. "I have bigger fish to fry," he said, me being a minnow. He would drink a beer before his postgame news conference and then he'd belch the beer while talking to us. That's my interpretation. I didn't like being around him then. He didn't like being around us.

At the beginning of his final season, the Warriors held a media day for us to interview the players and coaches. Afterward, Nelson came over to me. He was smiling shyly.

"Do you want to play shuffleboard at Smitty's over on Grand Avenue?" he asked.

Shuffleboard, that board game you see in bars. Word was Don Nelson bought the shuffleboard table for Smitty's and went there with his dog. Every alarm rang in my head when he invited me. I told myself, *Be careful, he's trying to weasel me again.* He was giving me a watch, asking for a source's name.

"I'd really like to go, Don," I said, "but I have to meet my wife for lunch."

He knew I was lying and he knew why. And the season dribbled out and we never even said goodbye to each other.

Several years later, the Warriors invited a few reporters to an intimate lunch with Nelson, who was visiting Oakland from his home in Hawaii. He and I had not spoken after he left the Warriors. The lunch was at the Oakland Marriott, a long table with Nelson at the head. I sat immediately to his left. He looked thin and fit and seemed happy away from the NBA. He told us about his house right on the ocean, bragged about a shave ice stand he ran in town, told us about his poker games with Willie Nelson, Woody Harrelson, and Owen Wilson.

After a while, I said I was leaving and started to rise. He gently put his hand on my arm, motioned for me to sit. He leaned over to me, whispered for only the two of us to hear: "You never did play shuffleboard with me that time when I asked you."

I thought he had forgotten all about it. I sure had. I felt emotional. He looked sad. I never saw him look like that before. I drew the conclusion that he really wanted to play shuffleboard that afternoon, was sincere, had no other agenda. Just two guys hanging out. He saw his career ending, his life entering its final phase, and he wanted to spend a few hours with an old-timer who knew him when.

That could have been true. Or was Nellie being Nellie again? You got me.

DRAWING THE LINE:
DESPERATE AT DEADLINE

I T'S NIGHT GAMES WHEN I WANT TO VOMIT.

At night games, deadline becomes an enemy, a raging beast—the dead-line there in the real world, the raging beast there in my head.

You've probably never thought about deadline, emphasis on *dead*, but consider this. If a writer misses deadline—is late—the copy editor can't read the copy on time and release the edited article to the layout person who releases the completed section for printing so the delivery trucks can grab the papers on schedule and deliver them.

A writer misses deadline, everything backs up, and that means overtime pay up and down the line. Management wants to have papers in people's driveways by 6:00 A.M. or in stacks at the 7-Eleven where people can grab a paper and a cup of coffee on their way to work. Miss a deadline by, say, fifteen minutes—the guy leaves home without the paper. He drives home sore because he didn't read his paper and he probably drives across it still lying in the driveway and gets double sore. Or the guy at the 7-Eleven gets his coffee without the paper. These are the worries that make circulation managers drink.

You miss deadline and you get a rebuke from management or maybe a note in your personnel file, or the editor subs some AP article where your story was supposed to be—a humiliation, a curse, a professional judgment of failure.

Because night games finish late, I feel deadline pressure the minute I enter the ballpark or arena. At the *Press Democrat*, the deadline used to be 10:30 P.M. The paper has raised the deadline to 11:00 P.M., thank God. That half hour is years in writing time. At the *Chronicle*, the deadline was around 6:00 P.M. for the bulldog edition—the early paper. Impossible to file from a game no one has played. I used to write an early column on another subject, just in case, then the desk would kill it when my *real* column came in.

Let's use the *Press Democrat*'s 10:30 P.M. deadline as a benchmark, see how that plays out in real time.

Baseball is the worst.

Why?

Because there's no clock. Theoretically, a game could go on forever. When a night game enters extra innings, God forbid, you hear heavy groaning in press row. I expect to see writers hurl themselves out the window in a mass suicide. No columnists in their right minds cover a regular-season night game. That changes in the postseason when columnists must be there. They should assign a psychiatrist to the press box for emergency interventions.

Monday Night Football is another writer killer because it starts late. And ends late. And almost all Golden State Warriors games are murder because, at home, the Warriors usually tip off at around 7:40 P.M. That leaves two hours and fifty minutes for the game and the writing. I am in trouble before I even start.

The Warriors are double-trouble because they're an elite team. A columnist must cover them in the regular season. No excuses like, "I have a great story on technological advances in shoelaces that takes precedence over the game." No way. I start writing before the game based on some comment coach Steve Kerr made in his pregame media get-together. Even if I don't end up using pregame Kerr, his quotes give me confidence—I have words on screen. Maybe two hundred words.

There is one immutable sports-writing truth: *Words equal time.*

Words may convey facts and words may tell a story and words may be beautiful and words were what Shakespeare used. Well, screw all that, and screw Shakespeare and the iambic pentameter he rode in on. For a desperate deadline writer, words equal time.

I have to write, say, nine hundred words by deadline. I have two hundred in the bank. That saves ten minutes at the end. In writing time, ten minutes is an eon.

So, I have two hundred not-very-good words, and the game starts and I immediately start writing. I'm writing stuff that happens in the first quarter knowing I'll probably kill it. I write it anyway, hoping it holds up. I write and kill and write and kill. I am watching the game and I am writing and killing and my head bobs up and down. I am a bobblehead.

The game ends and I have about five hundred words, if I'm lucky. I may even have my lead and a strong focus. But it's ten o'clock. Sometimes, it's 10:10. My press box meal is rising in my throat. I rush down to the interview room hoping Kerr is brilliant. I bring my computer and type his words as he speaks, squeeze in his quotes where they fit in the story.

This is writing?

I rush into the locker room like a madman, hoping to get a scrap of a quote from Draymond Green or Stephen Curry if they're not killing time in the shower. Then I flee to the press room and knock out four hundred more words in fifteen or twenty minutes, saying to myself, "Please don't let this be a JFG column"—Just Fucking Gibberish. The only consolation? Everyone else is fucked like me.

It can get worse. Often does. Warriors games can be close until the end. Tick-tock, ticktock. Sure, if the Warriors wallop the Lakers, if the game is over by halftime, I have an unbeatable sense of well-being. Own the world. Take my time in the press section while the game unfolds. Find the right words, maybe some snappy metaphors. But the game could come down to the wire. When it's certain the game will be a nail-biter, when I realize this in the third quarter, I resort to the line. Draw the line on my screen. The line looks like this.

The line is my salvation and my curse and it calls my professional integrity into question.

On top of the line, I write a Warriors-win-the-game column. Below the line, I write a Warriors-lose-the-game column. Remember I need at least five hundred words when the game ends. I can't risk five hundred words on the wrong topic—a Warriors-win column when the Warriors end up losing or vice versa. Professional suicide.

So, I write two columns at the same time while I'm also watching the game and taking notes. Every other columnist is facing the same cruel reality. Every other columnist is suffering and sighing and snorting. Every other columnist is writing two self-canceling columns. Maybe they use the line. Maybe they don't. I've never asked. I'm hyperventilating just recalling those days.

Above the line, I write a few paragraphs explaining how the Warriors showed their championship grit by "gutting out" a close win at the end and I praise Stephen Curry for being a great "leader." I leave room in the text for his final point total. I present him as the Christ child incarnate.

Every few minutes, I dip below the line and write a competing column claiming the Warriors didn't have the stomach to hold off the surging Lakers who took over as the final buzzer approached. I criticize Curry for throwing away the ball at crucial moments and question his poise and leadership going into the playoffs. Yes, I question his leadership even though in the Warriors-win column I praise it.

Although the columns absolutely contradict each other, I thoroughly believe both of them. I have to. I believe the Warriors are very good and not so good. I believe Curry is a leader and not a leader. When the game ends, when the issue is decided, I simply delete the irrelevant column, also deleting my false belief. In my semi-crazed state, sometimes I forget how to delete the line I drew. *The desk guys will handle that*, I tell myself. I grab my computer and run to the media room.

I need to mention the Gonzalez.

In the early 1970s, when I attended Stanford, some friends and I decided to drive from the Bay Area to Mexico. In one day. We aimed for Ensenada or Rosarito Beach. I don't remember which. We headed out in the afternoon. Didn't think things through. Like time and distance. It was late by the time we passed LA so, what the hell, we stopped at a motel near the freeway, woke up the poor guy at the front desk—he looked mortally offended—and we rented a room. The next day we drove to Ensenada or Rosarito Beach and got there in plenty of time.

We were walking around town buying huaraches and sombreros and other stuff and noticed a worn-out motel down a dirt road. It was called the Gonzalez. My friends said, "Let's make a reservation at the Gonzalez."

"That place?!" I said. "It's a dump. We'll find a better motel later. Trust me."

Later, we trudged from motel to motel. No vacancies. Swallowing hard, I said, "What about the Gonzalez?"

No vacancy.

We ended up driving back across the border and went to the same motel from the night before. Woke up the same poor guy. He seemed mortally offended.

What does the Gonzalez have to do with deadline writing and above the line and below the line? Just this. When you're desperate, all your standards vanish. In the afternoon, the Gonzalez wasn't good enough for me. In the dark and with no options, it was the Taj Mahal.

Same with above- and below-the-line writing. I let all my standards disappear as the clock moves forward and the game doesn't resolve itself. I write sentences I wouldn't accept from Dick and Jane, go to Cliché City. I write the team that won "wanted it more." I write about "character" as the deciding factor. This is all bullshit but I've fallen way below the Gonzalez Line.

In the locker room, I welcome any horrible quote.

"We play them one at a time."

"We work hard as a team and that's why we won."

"Sure, we lost, but it's just one game. It'll make us tougher."

I use quotes like those and love them. Total Gonzalez.

Is it ethical to write two contradictory columns? Is it ethical to believe both of them? Is it ethical to write crummy prose on deadline and accept the lousiest quotes? I have asked myself these questions hundreds of times. I always come up with the same answer: Who the hell cares about philosophical niceties at a time like that? Shit, I made deadline.

33

PRIAPIC FIXATION:
ATHLETES AND
THEIR DOINKERS

W HEN MARK JACKSON COACHED the Golden State Warriors for three seasons starting in 2011, he presented himself as a holy man. In news conferences, he lectured the media about God and once even said his team was touched by the hand of the Creator.

Not that I cared about Jackson's religious beliefs or if the Warriors were touched by Jehovah. I was there to cover hoops, not Jackson's theology. I would attend Jackson news conferences and wonder what was so special about the Warriors in a metaphysical sense. Why weren't the Celtics or the Knicks or the Cavaliers touched by God? Or the Lakers. I've always worried that these God spielers suffer from the sin of pride. But I could have lived with Jackson's spiel and his pride. It was his hypocrisy that was the living end.

Allow me to be more specific. The living end with Mark Jackson was his penis, his schlong, his dick, his dingus, his ding-dong, joystick, peter, chub-bie, boner, hard-on, Mr. Winky, pickle, one-eyed monster, pee-pee, putz, lizard, wanker, and, of course, his schvantz.

Jackson may be a very holy man. He preached at True Love Worship Center International in Van Nuys, California, along with his wife Desiree. But his trouser snake, python, cobra, not to mention his Chairman Mao, once got him in trouble, a fate visited on many unsuspecting men.

During his tenure as Warriors coach, the news broke that Jackson had sent pictures of his Kielbasa six years earlier to a stripper with whom he was having an affair, even though he was happily married at the time. Years after the affair ended, the stripper and a male accomplice, being the kind of people they were, said they would go public with Jackson's johnson photo unless he paid up. Jackson realized he had been careless with his genitalia and forked over five grand. The extortionists weren't satisfied and wanted more. At that point, Jackson called in the FBI on wang-dang-doodle patrol. There was a sting. The extortionists got caught. And Jackson got caught with, well, his pants down.

Fine. It could happen in the best of families, and Jackson always seemed like an honorable man. But I knew that one thing about him. He once had shown his pecker and whenever he became serious with the media, especially about his personal relationship with the Deity, I imagined him snapping a photo of his schmeckel and sending it to the stripper. I wanted to die laughing, like when some blowhard lectures you about proper etiquette, except he has a glob of spinach stuck in his teeth. I would listen to the preacher Jackson and think, "Excuse me, Mark. I'm supposed to take you seriously?"

How does a man, even the holiest of men, maintain the pious stance with his fly unzipped?

And he wasn't the only one sending out salami photos. Draymond Green of the Warriors disseminated his own dick pic on Snapchat. At first, Green said he had been hacked, the usual opening gambit of a social-media screwup. But being the upright man he is, Green manned up, rose up, became a stand-up guy, and admitted he meant to send the doinker photo privately but hit the wrong button. Note: When you absolutely need to send a photo of your willy, it's essential to hit the right button.

And then there was former New York congressman Anthony Weiner who got caught sexting photos of his own weiner, at least one to an underage girl. Never has a man been more appropriately named. Weiner's weiner shots cost him his political career and marriage.

Re: the weiner. Here's a personal story. When my son was five years old, he walked into the kitchen where my wife and I were washing the dinner dishes.

"Dad," he said in his little-boy voice, "when you had me did you have to put your weiner in Mom's *bagina*?" Bagina with a B.

I looked at my wife for help. She shrugged, which meant, *You're on your own, Buster.*

I stared at my son, me with a stricken face, and said, "Yes, I put my weiner in Mom's vagina." Satisfied, he left the kitchen. A few minutes later, he came back, his innocent face full of curiosity.

"Did you ever have to do it again?"

I told him we'd talk when he was older.

But he was five. Jackson, Green, and Weiner were considerably older when the weiner fixation overtook them. I've concluded a subgroup of men exists, men who proudly send out photos of their schmucks. Call them Schmucks of America.

All hail.

34

FANS

FANS SAY *WE* AND *US*. This is when they talk about the teams they root for. Fans think they are part of the team, part of the team's family. Teams encourage this bullshit because it creates loyalty and loyalty sells season tickets and the teams make money.

Professional sports are about money from top to bottom.

When I talk to fans and they start calling a team *us*, I want to set them straight. They are not part of the team. The whole team family thing is a myth. To me the team is not us, but I was a sports writer. I was not part of the fan world. In my world, the team is the *other*, something out there, and it has no emotional standing in my life. If fans want to be we-us people, find meaning in their relationship with the team, that's their business. And God love them for it.

When I talk to fans, they constantly tell me what's wrong with the team, what the team needs, or why the team is great. They explain why I'm wrong for criticizing the team even if it has a bad record. They say it's unfair to report controversial news—I'm being negative and not helping the team.

I want to say, but I don't say: It's not my job to help the team. The team needs to help itself.

I want to say, but don't say: When an editor asks me to get fan reaction, I refuse. I don't care what fans think. Sorry, I don't. I can't stand when TV announcers tell us, "The crowd needs to get involved." Meaning the home fans have to shout a lot. Professional athletes don't need fans to be involved, don't need fans shouting to make them play better. Professional athletes earn millions to play well in an empty gym, if it comes to that.

When fans tell me what's going on with a team, I want to ask, but don't ask: Whom do you know with inside knowledge? Where have you been to observe the inner workings of the team? Have you spent hours reporting from the locker room or clubhouse, hanging around, putting in your time, sometimes subjected to rudeness from athletes? What source have you met privately to learn the deep-down truth—not merely the appearance? Are you detached from the team, able to make dispassionate judgments? Or do you feel angry, sad, elated depending on how the team plays? Are you personally involved with the team's record? Do you have something at stake?

I want to ask all these questions, but I never do. Fans need to be fans and I don't wish to be rude. Mostly, I smile and then look away.

35

FIFTEEN %: THE TOTAL TONNAGE OF WHAT WE DON'T KNOW ABOUT ATHLETES

T HE WORST THING a sports writer can call another sports writer is *fan*. It usually comes out he or she is "a fucking fan." *Fan* applied to another writer is a curse word. It means the writer roots for the team he covers, has lost objectivity, is unprofessional, a pimp.

When people found out I wrote sports—not something I advertised—they often asked if I rooted for the Bay Area teams. They expected me to say yes. I said no. I said becoming a sports writer means giving up being a fan. Letting go of all those feelings of joy and loss. I said being a sports writer is like being the harem eunuch.

People didn't believe me. "Come on, you can admit it," they'd say. "You root for the [Raiders/49ers/Giants/Athletics/Warriors—fill in the team's name]." I couldn't convince them. In their minds, I was a fan.

When the San Francisco Giants won a World Series, a childhood friend wrote an email congratulating me. He is a college professor. I wrote back and said congratulations weren't in order. I didn't play for the Giants, wasn't in their organization, didn't get a World Series share or a ring. I told him the Giants winning or losing was irrelevant to me. I had to write about them one way or another, didn't get anything from a World Series win except the painful assignment to cover the victory parade.

When people understood that I didn't care if a local team won, they would ask why I wrote sports. What was the point? And I said I liked to write about sports, understood that world. Simple as that. I was a writer and I loved describing the beauty of shortstop Brandon Crawford diving to his right for a ground ball, picking it up and gunning the throw to first base. And I loved bringing up a subject to start a discussion or an argument among readers. Does Barry Bonds belong in the Hall of Fame? No, he does not. It's what a columnist does, starts people talking. I enjoyed being that catalyst. But I was just as happy if the local teams won or lost. I had zero stake in their success. Was detached, as I was supposed to be.

As a sports writer I disappointed fans in other ways. When people learned I was a sports writer, the holy glow took over their eyes. The way ancient Hebrews looked when they gazed at Moses. Moses was deemed worthy of talking to God and I talked to ballplayers, the representatives of God on Earth.

People—and I mean most people, men and women—didn't care about me. Not for myself. They cared that I went to the hallowed place—the clubhouse or locker room.

"Oh, you meet the players," people said to me hundreds of times. Meeting the players, a form of being anointed by God. And after I admitted that, yes, I did, people asked—always asked—what is so-and-so like?

Here's a painful fact. Meeting the players is no special fun, not for a journalist. That's what I always wanted to say, but I restrained myself. You don't tell a true believer God can be an asshole.

Why is meeting the players no fun?

Because players and media don't get along. Or if they get along, the transaction is tense and guarded, especially on the players' part. They have so much to lose from a careless word, an unguarded moment. You ask a player for his time and you can see the wariness in him—not always, but often. You are the enemy. To be safe, they say the minimum. Especially in football where public-relations people monitor interviews and routinely cut off reporters. You feel like you're in maximum security lockup talking to players on a phone and looking at them through fortified glass.

I remember the 49ers locker room after midweek practices. The media would be allowed in for an hour or so at lunchtime. Most players hid in an off-limits room. The locker room would be empty, a wasteland, except for maybe the kickers and an offensive lineman or two hanging around their lockers. Not the star players. The writers would talk among themselves. Everyone knew the national media broke the big stories—who was traded, who was in the doghouse. It sure seemed management catered to the national media instead of the local people. And who could blame management? The national press had more power and the local people seemed vestigial.

So when people would ask, "What is Alex Smith or Derek Carr like?" I didn't have the slightest idea. I knew how they presented themselves to the media—cheerful, optimistic, polite, professional. But I never spent time with them away from games or practices. They didn't visit my house. I didn't visit theirs. You don't really know people until you or they cross the home threshold.

Even in the 1980s and 1990s, when athletes were more accessible, I hardly knew them. I spoke to Joe Montana often, but it was about football. And he was especially careful with me. Still is, even though we're both retired. Steve Young always was cheerful and warm and I think he was sincere. Did I really know Ronnie Lott?

I adhered to the 15-Percent Rule. I knew 15 percent about a player. Tops. In most cases the number hovered near zero. I never wanted players as friends. How do you tell a team to trade a friend? How do you call out a friend for dropping a pass or booting a ground ball or dogging it down the first-base line? How are you ruthlessly honest about a friend?

So, yes, I got 15 percent and was satisfied with that.

36

WHAT JOE THEISMANN DOESN'T KNOW ABOUT ALBERT EINSTEIN

B EFORE WE GOT THE GIGGLES, we were listening politely to former Washington Redskins quarterback Joe Theismann, who was talking to us at the Metrodome in Minneapolis a few days before Super Bowl XXVI. That's Super Bowl 26, January 1992, which the Redskins would win 37–24 over the Buffalo Bills. The listeners were San Francisco Bay Area sports columnist Ann Killion and me, and it was Media Day and we were asking Theismann about Redskins head coach Joe Gibbs, for whom Theismann had played.

We asked Theismann if Gibbs was a genius. Remember we covered the 49ers. Their legendary coach Bill Walsh was known as "The Genius," among other things, and Gibbs was at Walsh's level. Theismann considered our question, shook his head, and emphatically shot back—and I'll never forget this—"Nobody in the game of football should be called a genius. A genius is somebody like Norman Einstein."

You know that feeling when electricity sparks between you and another person. Sparks flying between the two of you. Ann and I were in electric shock. Had Joe Theismann just said Norman freaking Einstein? Did he really not know the theory of relativity guy was named Albert?

Ann and I couldn't look at each other. We didn't dare. If we did, I might have fallen on the ground and writhed in laughter or peed my pants. So, we stared at our notebooks and pretended to write, but our shoulders were violently shaking and we were snorting with laughter. I definitely remember Ann snorting. Theismann, aware we were laughing at him—how could he not be?—said, "I'll be back in a minute," and fled. He didn't come back.

At which point Ann and I could breathe again. Took honking deep breaths. She had tears in her eyes. Laughter tears. We both wrote columns about Theismann and Norman Einstein. We'd be nuts not to. I made fun of Theismann. I'm sorry, Joe. I posited Norman was Albert's smarter brother, that Norman, not Albert, was the one who did all the complicated thinking. Albert was a mere front man for the brother act. The whole point was Theismann was a dope or maybe he took so many head shots he didn't know the difference between an Albert and a Norman. The story of Theismann and Norman Einstein got picked up all over America, including by *Sports Illustrated*. And there the matter stood for years, Theismann as the guy who didn't know Albert Einstein's name.

Several years later, I was in Manhattan covering some game or other. A friend invited me to dinner at Palm Too, a great New York steak joint on Second Avenue. Large group around a big table, mostly sports writers except for two men I didn't know. We drank, got lubricated, and I talked with the two strangers. They said they had gone to high school at South River High in South River, New Jersey, and Theismann was their classmate.

Cue the laugh track. I told the Theismann Norman Einstein story expecting to get a howl, expecting them to say Theismann was a douchebag or something like that. Not the case. Both grew serious. With reverence in their voices they said there indeed was a Norman Einstein. And they knew him. Everyone knew him. He had been valedictorian at South River High and the whole school respected his big brain, including Theismann. Norman Einstein had become a doctor. What more did you need to know?

Well, that changed everything. Redeemed Theismann. He knew what he was talking about. Joe Gibbs might have been smart for a football coach, but he was no Norman Einstein. No one was. Not even that underachiever Albert.

37

SCREEN SNOOPERS:
PRESS BOX PLAGIARISTS

I T'S CREEPY. Some writer is behind you, walking back and forth in the press
box. Walking slowly. Very slowly.

You know what's happening. You're in the presence of a screen snooper.
You hunch over your computer, blocking the screen. The snooper slows down.
You imagine him (it could be a her) straining to see what you've written. You
turn around quickly, the snooper is startled. Hustles away.

Caught.

Or the snooper can be a leaner-inner. Snoopers are creative. Snooper walks
over, puts his hand on your back, begins cordial chatting. Like you're friends.
Forget you're on deadline. The snooper talks. You feel his breath on your neck,
get the mouth-smell of the brat he ate for lunch. He leans over your shoulder
and stares at your screen. Blatant. You pull down the screen on your laptop,
blocking snooper's view. He pretends not to notice. Stops talking. Walks away.

Screen snoopers—other writers know who they are—are idea thieves. They want to see your lead. Because they don't have a lead. They want to know if you are breaking news. It could be a tip from a player. The snooper wants your tip.

I bet you've known a snooper. He cheated off you on the high-school history final, pretended to drop his pencil, leaned over to copy your answers. Okay, so you know it happens. People cheat on history finals. But the press-box snooper chose this profession. It's his passion. He sure didn't become a sports writer for the money. And he's cheating? You want to say, *Look at your own fucking screen.* You want to say, *I sure wouldn't copy off a loser like you.*

The snooper is advertising, *I suck at my job.* He wants you to know he sucks. No pride. But you're not responsible for the snooper's desperation. You're responsible for your own desperation. Your desperation is all you can handle.

Sometimes you're late for a group interview with a player or coach. Traffic tie-up. It happens. Other writers give you a transcript of the quotes. You do the same for them. Sharing group quotes with writers from other papers is a professional courtesy. The snooper never shares, not even with writers at his own paper. He is greedy. He takes, won't give.

Snoopers can snoop without snooping. Eighth inning of a close game, snooper walks over to a writer from another paper, someone with no obligation to the snooper. Snooper says, "What's today's topic?" As if it's a group enterprise. As if writers from all papers, as competitive as athletes, pool their ideas. Most writers are polite when the screen snooper begs for an idea. I've heard others say, "Get out of my fucking face."

Some snoopers are aural. You're having a conversation with someone from your paper. It could be beat writer and columnist. You talk in whispers, divvying up material. You don't want to broadcast this. Somehow the aural snooper is there. Always there. Inclines his head toward you, pretending not to eavesdrop. Tries to catch a phrase, a clue. Later, you see him writing in his notebook.

Snooping leads to problems of etiquette. You're writing on deadline. You need to use the washroom. As you walk away, you ask yourself, "Do I leave my screen up?"

If you leave it up, somebody can read your copy. Leaving your screen up makes you vulnerable. If you shut it, you're just about accusing your neighbor of being a cheater—he may not be a cheater but you can't be sure. If you pull down your screen, you're boasting, "My work is so good people want to steal my ideas." Pull down your screen, you lack trust.

Who asked for this dilemma? What would Miss Manners say?

I usually left my screen up unless I sat next to a known snooper. I gave people the benefit of the doubt.

Non-snoopers want to get even with snoopers. I know one who did. Brilliantly.

An out-of-town team was playing a series against the Dodgers in LA. A beat writer covering the visiting team got to the ballpark early. Baseball writers arrive three hours before a game. Sometimes four hours, and they work three hours after the game. Long days. Hard work. This beat writer—call him Writer One—knew a writer for another paper—call him Writer Two—was chronically late to the ballpark. Lazy. Writer One knew Writer Two would panic, afraid he'd missed something, and then he'd snoop. Writer One wanted to get even with Writer Two for past snooping transgressions.

He set a trap. Wrote a complete phony article, a made-up story saying two early arriving players for the visiting team had fought in the clubhouse before that night's game. Threw punches. There were headlocks. Teammates had to separate them. Writer One even invented quotes from players and the manager, veered off to total fiction. Admirable work. Then Writer One walked out of the press box, leaving his screen in the up position, available to be read. Left it up on purpose.

After that, Writer One went into the visitors' clubhouse and told the other writers what he'd done. Call them Writers Three, Four, Five, etc. They knew the deal. They'd suspected Writer Two, as well. They wanted proof. They wanted justice.

The writers waited for the snooper. He dashed into the clubhouse a half hour later, terror smeared across his face. He had missed something big by being late, needed to catch up. He ran to one of the "combatants." Asked what started the fight. Player looked at him like he was nuts. "There was no fight," player said. Writer Two pressed the player about the fight, assumed he was hiding the truth, saving face. Player told him to get lost. Writer Two hurried to the other "combatant." Asked about the fight. "What fight?" Writer Two wouldn't give up. Player told him to take a hike. Writer Two approached other players, asked about the fight. All denied a fight. Finally, he hurried into the manager's office, asked about the fight. Manager stared at him. "There was no fight," manager shouted. "Where are you getting this?" Writer Two wrote that in his notebook. Other writers watched him, laughed their asses off.

Writer Two's game story that night focused on the fight that wasn't a fight. He wrote that, contrary to a report, two players did not punch it out. He called the other article erroneous and implied Writer One was unprofessional.

But, of course, there was no report and there was no erroneous article because Writer One had eliminated the fictitious story by simply pressing delete.

38

BREAKING THE ICE: TIM LINCECUM FEELS EMBARRASSED

TIM LINCECUM TURNED HIS BACK TO THE CLUBHOUSE. He was staring into his locker, his shoulders hunched. The body language clear: stay away.

It was a warning to the media, not to his teammates. Lincecum was a good teammate. He didn't like the media. That's what he thought. But he really did like the media. Once he got talking, it was like a psychotherapy session; Lincecum amazingly admitted his deepest fears about his declining ability, his declining velocity, his declining results. He had a small body and he had given everything, thrown pitches with his arm and his heart, and now he neared the end.

So, in spring training 2015, his final season with the San Francisco Giants, he turned his back. It was early morning at Scottsdale Stadium in Arizona and the players were wandering into the clubhouse. Some were sleepily sipping coffee. The room was quiet. Near Lincecum one player shouted into his cell phone, "I never called you a bitch!"

I wanted to interview Lincecum. The reason I was there at 8:00 A.M. How do you interview a man with his back turned and his shoulders hunched? Any move toward him would be an intrusion, even a simple, "Excuse me, Tim. Got a minute?"

I left the clubhouse frustrated. Also feeling I had failed because I didn't have the guts to interrupt whatever it was Lincecum was doing. Or not doing. I stood in a hallway outside the clubhouse trying to appear busy, pretending I was accomplishing something. I read the lists pasted on the wall—the lineups, the workout schedules—but they were irrelevant to me. Just past me was the players' eating room where the Giants could go for eggs, cereal, and juice. Several players walked by me all engulfed in silence. Here came Lincecum. This was an opening. And I almost took it, but as he ducked into the eating room he also ducked his eyes. And I lost my voice or my nerve, and once again hated myself.

Finally, he reappeared, walked in my direction, didn't look at me. As he came close, I said—and I don't know where this came from—"Tim, may I have a few minutes or should I just go fuck myself?"

He stopped. Stared at me. The most surprised look on his young innocent face. Or maybe it was a look of disappointment. In me.

"I would never tell you to do that," he said, his voice gentle.

I think I blushed. He led me to his locker. Gave me an interview. Atoned for my cynical view of human nature and, certainly, of him. Took that upon himself. Took everything upon himself.

39

WHAT BRUCE BOCHY
WON'T SAY

S AN FRANCISCO GIANTS MANAGER BRUCE BOCHY never used my name.
Let me amend that. Never used it in public. I realized this just before
I retired in January 2017. And it astonished me.

I would ask a question, he would nod and reply. This was in group interviews where I was one of the crowd. He wouldn't acknowledge he knew
me. Wouldn't acknowledge we had worked together for years. Wouldn't acknowledge we had talked off the record. Wouldn't acknowledge me.

And I respected that.

Bochy was an old-style manager with the press. He honored tradition.
His first duty was to beat writers, the people who covered his team daily (including road games), who lost sleep making early-morning flights after night
games, who arrived at the ballpark hours before the game, did due diligence
in the clubhouse and manager's office, and who left the park hours after a

night game, tired and disheveled, and grabbed a crummy meal at a twenty-four-hour coffee shop, and came to the ballpark the next day and did it again.

With beat writers, Bochy was all first name. Andy and Alex and Janie and Chris and Henry. He was deferential and patient, a professional honoring other professionals doing their jobs.

I was never a baseball beat writer. I was a columnist covering several sports, often dividing my attention in baseball season between the Giants and Oakland A's, Raiders and 49ers. I was a generalist, not a specialist. I traveled with the Giants only in the playoffs. In the regular season, I would come to the ballyard once or twice a week strictly for day games. I appeared on a drop-in basis. When I showed up, I would occasionally hear beat writers mutter the word *fraud*, meaning me. Meaning all columnists. Because we did not put in the time. In spring training, some of the beat writers in the press box would stack two plastic chairs, one on the other, for a better view of the field. Like thrones. That left no chair for me, a fraud, and I had to scrounge one from the media eating room.

Bochy never denied me a chair, but he denied me a name. For him I was a second-level baseball writer. Maybe third-level. And he was right. I was peripheral in his world. Privately it was Lowell this and Lowell that, but publicly he would not first-name me.

Which meant we had a working relationship, nothing more. I liked that. I could criticize him without feeling disloyal, not that he deserved criticism when I covered him. He won three World Series. With Bochy, I mostly interacted with the manager who spoke before games. That persona. But it was a persona only—just like the doctor who puts on his smile face as he enters the examination room, becomes The Doctor for the patient. Doing his job. Putting on a professional front.

People would ask, "What's Bochy like?" I'd shrug. I had known Giants managers Frank Robinson and Roger Craig. They always Lowelled me. And across the Bay at the A's, I knew Tony La Russa, Art Howe, Ken Macha, Bob Melvin, and even general manager Billy Beane. Especially Billy Beane. Not Bochy.

Bochy could be hard on coaches. That's what I was told. I never saw it. He liked to tour the wine country. I never toured with him. I once wrote about his love of wine. A big-deal winery sent him a case of expensive stuff based on my article. Bochy thanked me without using my name in a media group, asked if I could get him a red pickup truck.

Not knowing Bochy, not *really* knowing people I knew on the surface, was a feeling I came to appreciate.

I never knew Golden State Warriors coach Steve Kerr. The media thinks they know him, are close to him, share a relationship with him. They think he cares about them. To which I say, "Maybe."

He is unremittingly friendly. A thoroughly decent man from what I observed—my observations were limited to a certain context. He knows people's names. Makes jokes. Is quick-witted and pleasant and nice. Very nice. But this, too, is a persona. It's how he handles the media, gets us on his side—to his credit. I never had a meaningful conversation with him. Never shared anything besides basketball. When people ask what Kerr is like, I say, "You got me." He would be surprised I have his cell number. I'm a journalist. I get those things. I never phoned him, never called and said, "How's it hanging, Steve?" Or, "Seen any good movies lately?" I see him behind a pane of glass, right there but not right there.

Only once did he emerge from behind the glass, when the Warriors lost to the Cavaliers in the 2016 NBA Finals. Not until the next season—preseason actually—did I have a chance to ask Kerr what went wrong. I asked in a group, asked what he learned from the loss. He answered in generalities, brushed me off. I hung in there like he wants his players to hang in on defense, asked him to be specific—fulfilling my job to ask a follow-up, to solicit particular examples. He turned his face away from me, didn't say a word.

Revealing? I think so. Not sure how.

I liked interviewing managers, coaches, general managers, team CEOs, and owners. They grew old along with me, evolved and changed. Ballplayers—name the sport—usually fall into the demographic age range of twenty to thirty-five. They never grow older, just change names and uniform numbers. I found conversation with them redundant, often unsatisfying because, generally, they were not worldly and mostly thought about their sport and themselves. Of course, there were exceptions. I asked players about baseball, football, basketball, etc. I needed to. But to get an understanding of the team or write about a person with depth, I went to a coach or executive.

Like the A's general manager Billy Beane. A complicated character up there with Don Nelson. A good-guy, bad-guy like Nelson. With Beane you can have a relationship of sorts. If he's pissed at something you wrote, he yells at you. You yell back. Out in the open. He did okay putting together a team for a cheap crummy ownership, always getting rid of players to keep salaries down. Beane is smart, maybe brilliant. His managers—some of them anyway—had a love-hate relationship with him. At times hate-hate. He would barge into the manager's office after a game and shout and scream about one thing or another. This could be after a win. He didn't like how the manager won. Didn't apply A's baseball philosophy. One manager, a good man, told me he wanted to deck Billy.

Beane was complicit in making out the lineup card. He's a stats guy and has ideas who should play and who should hit where in the batting order based on certain metrics. The lineup card represents Beane's point of view along with the manager's. I never could imagine the Giants' Brian Sabean telling Bruce Bochy whom to play. Beane has the ultimate *chutzpah* and routinely demeaned manager Art Howe (see *Moneyball*); although later, after Howe had left the A's, Beane invited him back as a special advisor. Howe declined.

One time, I was alone with Beane in his office. Spring training. Beane wore shorts and a T-shirt and sandals. He put his cell phone on vibrate. It kept buzzing but he didn't interrupt the conversation or even look who'd called. Gave me his full attention. His dog, a border collie, walked around the office trying to herd us. It was a scene out of Norman Rockwell.

After the interview—an A-plus interview—I got up to leave. Beane stopped me. Would I stay? He had one question.

Sure, I said.

Had I ever been in the office of Giants general manager Brian Sabean at AT&T Park?

I said yes.

Beane asked what it was like. He was staring into my eyes. Really wanted to know. I said Sabean's office was nothing special. Just an office. A desk. Bookcases with media guides. Lots of printouts on his desk with lots of numbers. I remembered the room being neat.

Beane thought about that. We shook hands and I left, walked into the deserted stands in the early morning, and thought about Beane. How revealing his question was.

When I taught creative writing at University of San Francisco, I always gave a particular assignment. Describe a room associated with your main character. It could be a bedroom, office, etc. Do not tell who the character is. Let the description speak for itself. Let the description disclose the character.

And Beane had given me that assignment. He wanted to know Sabean through his office and his things. Thought the office would portray the in-ner Sabean, the essential Sabean. Of course, this meant Beane didn't know Sabean, although they had known each other for decades. It meant Beane never had been in Sabean's office, twenty miles away. It meant Beane had a fascination for Sabean, a silent, controlled man who revealed nothing of himself. Sabean had a smoldering fury. Never spoke to the whisper guys, the reporters from various Internet sites who wanted the inside scoop. Fuck that. Beane longed to understand Sabean.

And I realized, sitting in the stands in the clear, cool morning light, I didn't reveal Sabean to Beane, but Beane revealed himself to me. Brian Sabean never once asked me about Billy Beane's office.

BABY AMARONE:
BRUCE BOCHY KNOWS
FROM WINE

S AN FRANCISCO GIANTS MANAGER BRUCE BOCHY usually kept his door closed before and after games, an office with a desk, two chairs, and a couch. If the door was open, it meant he was open for visitors, mostly sports writers.

When I saw the open door, I went in because here was an opportunity to oil the machine, keep the conversation going. I would sit on the couch and stare across the room at what looked like a refrigerator. But it wasn't a refrigerator. It was a wine humidifier and it was big as a refrigerator because, contrary to his working-class image, Bochy loves wine, has the most refined taste. He would proudly invite me to open the humidifier and search through his bottles, mostly powerful Napa cabernet sauvignons. A big man with a big head and a big taste.

He would tell me what he'd been drinking lately with dinner and ask what I was drinking. Two sports guys talking wine. One time I told him I just drank a baby Amarone, a milder version of Amarone, a flavorful, earthy, expensive red produced near Verona, Italy. Amarone means the Great Bitter, an indication of its robust, tannic taste.

"You ever hear of baby Amarone, Bruce?" I asked.

"Sure," he said with a big grin, "I drink that shit all the time."

HIGH-QUALITY
SPORTS BULLSHIT

T HE ULTIMATE INSINCERE PHRASE sports figures use when they get in trouble or caught doing the wrong thing and want an easy way out without taking blame or facing a single consequence, the one utterance that should result in a cream pie in the face or a one-thousand-dollar fine or both:

"I take full responsibility."

*****

Number Two on the all-time-insincere phrase list: A team executive gets fired but the team allows him to pretend he's leaving on his own. In a press release he asserts, cross his heart, hope to die:

"I'm leaving to spend more time with my family."

OVERALL AND
OTHER BAD WORDS

A COPY EDITOR CORRECTED MY COLUMN. I had written some player or other was the first player taken in the NFL draft. The sentence seemed perfectly clear to me. The editor phoned me at home, did me the courtesy of not messing with my prose without telling me.

He said "first player taken" was incorrect. He said the proper form was "the first overall player taken in the draft." The adjective *overall* held great significance for him. I assume he'd heard TV announcers say *overall* thousands of times and it seemed the correct usage to him, not that TV announcers worry much about the precision of words. He said there was an alternate way to write it. "So-and-So was the number-one overall pick in the draft."

He was insistent about *overall*.

It didn't seem like a big deal to me and, overall, I could live with his fix. But I didn't like it. I said *overall* didn't add anything to the sentence. Astonished, the editor asked why. I said because the first player taken in the draft meant the first player taken. First meant the first. Number One meant Number One. The word *overall* was redundant and unnecessary and, because American newspapers try to save space and reflect efficient, spare American prose, *overall* was wasteful.

The editor was sure of himself. It was the evening and I was eating dinner and I told him sure, okay, God love you, put in *overall* if it makes you happy. But I thought, God damn it, the first player taken is the first player taken and the fortieth player taken is the fortieth player taken, and *overall* is overmuch, and newspaper editors sometimes see life through heavy categories that weigh down prose. Or maybe it's just sports editors.

*****

And then there's *single*.

Not a sports word. An everybody word.

I keep hearing about the single biggest or the single greatest or the single worst. "This is the single worst tragedy to hit California in decades." As opposed to the "worst tragedy to hit California in decades."

The word *single* is a verbal stutter or a writing stutter. The worst means the worst. The *single* adds nothing to the thought.

Whenever I read something like "the single greatest basketball player," my heart flutters in a bad way, and I just shrug.

*****

And then there's, "He thought to himself," or, "She thought to herself." I hear and read this all the time: "'The waiter is pouring the wine with all the finesse of Dracula,' he thought to himself."

Need I explain?

43

MENSCH:
STEVE YOUNG AS USUAL

M Y SON WANTED TO MEET STEVE YOUNG. The 49ers had just won the Super Bowl in 1995 and Young had the greatest season up to that time of any quarterback ever, and my son was seven years old and believed in heroes.

I mentioned my son Grant to Young, how Grant longed to meet him. This was not easy for me. I kept my personal life and professional life separate, and even though I liked Young, as did most writers who covered him, we were not friends. Not in any way you'd call a person your friend. I covered him.

Young's eyes lit up. He said sure, bring him down to the facility, let's make a date. Which I did. My son wore a 49ers cap, too big for him—it slid down to his eyes—and he carried a reporter's notebook and a Sharpie. He was quiet on the drive from Oakland to Santa Clara. I could put myself in his place. Imagined myself at the age of seven driving somewhere to meet Duke Snider.

We parked the car and walked into the broad, high public area of 49ers headquarters, the room with Super Bowl trophies and an image of Marie De-Bartolo, mother of 49ers owner Eddie DeBartolo Jr. It looked like a cathedral and, in a way, it was. My son was speechless. I told the attendant we were here for Steve Young. The attendant said Young would appear shortly. Sit down in the waiting area.

There were two chairs facing each other. Grant—we called him Iggy—sat in my lap so Young could sit in the other chair. After a few minutes, Young came through a door. To say he *came* is incorrect. He *strode*. He *advanced*. He was a handsome young man in the fullness of his physical prime and we felt that and saw that. He wore shorts and a 49ers T-shirt, and his legs were muscled and his face was red with the blood of life. And he smiled because he understood what this meant to a boy.

He sat down in the chair and looked at me.

"Lowell, you sit there and don't say a word. This is between Iggy and me."

He sure knew how to create the moment. I shut up.

Young and Iggy made small talk. Iggy said he was a 49ers fan and Young nodded and grinned, although he must have heard that a million times. He asked Iggy what other sports he liked, tailored the conversation to a child, and I was grateful. After a while, Young said, "Iggy, do you have any questions for me?"

"Yes," Iggy said, surprisingly poised. "What does it feel like to throw a spiral?"

Young thought about that. "Look at my hand," he said. He moved his famous left hand toward Iggy, and Iggy held it. Looked at Young confused. What was Young getting at?

"My hand is small," Young said. "Joe has larger hands." He meant Joe Montana. "I love to throw perfect spirals, but I don't always because of my hand size," he said. "Sometimes, I throw an interception, but I leave the field happy because I threw a perfect spiral."

He and Iggy laughed. Young pointed to Iggy's cap. "Would you like me to sign it?" he asked. Iggy stared at Young. Moses seeing the burning bush. "Oh, yes," Iggy took off the cap and Young signed it, and I thought *It's time to leave.* But it wasn't.

"Do you want Jerry to sign your hat?" Young asked, meaning Jerry Rice.

Iggy's eyes lit up. "Yes," he said.

"Done," Young said. He took the cap and strode back through the door to the off-limits area.

Iggy and I waited a long time. Rice and I did not get along—we do now—and I imagined Young having to convince Rice to sign for Lowell Cohn's kid. After fifteen minutes, Young appeared, a frown on his face.

"I can't find Jerry," he said.

"Please don't worry about it," I said, trying to please, wanting not to make trouble, wanting not to impose or presume. The usual Jewish stuff. I moved Iggy off my lap and began to leave.

"No," Young almost shouted. "Don't go. I'll find Jerry. It may take a little time. That's what I wanted to tell you."

We sat down again. I felt rebuked. While we waited, tight end Brent Jones wandered by. I introduced Iggy, and Iggy said Steve was getting Jerry Rice to sign his cap. *Not on your life*, I thought. Jones said, "What about me? Can't I sign?" Now three of us waited for Young.

Young reappeared. "Jerry was eating lunch alone in a classroom," he said. He showed Iggy the cap with Rice's signature. Jones grabbed the cap and the Sharpie and he signed too. Iggy had scored. Then Jones and Young shook Iggy's hand and left and got back to work.

On the drive home, Iggy was thoughtful. So was I. I had come through as a father big-time, was proud of myself, felt like a hero. I had given Iggy something most fathers couldn't, and he would remember it his whole life and love me more for it.

Iggy looked at me, with an angelic smile on his face.

"Thank you," he said.

"Oh, you're welcome. It was a pleasure doing that for you."

"Just one thing," he said.

"What's that?" I asked in a confident, generous, everything-is-wonderful-with-the-world voice.

"I wish Steve was my dad."

DEATH OF SPARKY:
CHARLES M. SCHULZ
IN MEMORIAM

F EBRUARY 24, 2000.
 This is about the only time I met Charles Schulz, which happened
to be at his favorite hangout, the Redwood Empire Ice Arena in Santa
Rosa, California. I was writing a column for the *Santa Rosa Press Democrat*
about the Snoopy's Senior World Hockey Tournament, and I was told Schulz
would make time for me. Not that there was anything remarkable about that.
He would make time for anyone.

I was directed to meet him in the coffee shop of the ice arena, and
sure enough, when I got there, I saw him sitting alone at a table. He wore
a turtleneck, and his white hair was combed back from his face; with his
straight nose and elegant manner he might have been a US senator on
vacation. But of course, he was so much more important than that.

He invited me to sit down, after first saying, "Call me Sparky." So sure, I called him Sparky, but it felt weird. Like meeting FDR for the first time and calling him Frankie.

Then the interview began. Except I wasn't interviewing Schulz. He was interviewing me. His voice was soft, but he was persistent. He wanted to know everything about me—where I was from, when I came to the *Press Democrat*, why I write about sports. He was actually interested. It wasn't one of those perfunctory conversations in which the other guy goes through the motions of appearing polite but keeps checking his watch under the table and yawning behind his hand.

Schulz listened for a while, and then he said, "Where do you get your ideas for columns?"

I said there's usually lots of sports news I can write about. He nodded his head.

"Do you ever *not* have an idea?" he said.

"It feels like I don't have an idea about once a week," I told him.

He laughed. "Me, too," he said.

He thought for a moment. "And what do you do when you don't have an idea?" he asked.

"Well, that's a good question," I said. "Usually I can't sleep if I go to bed without an idea. I toss and turn and feel crummy, and my wife gets sore at me."

"Me, too," he said. "What happens next?"

"I wake up early with my heart pounding," I told him, "and I search the newspaper and listen to the radio to see if anything happened I can write about."

"And what if nothing happened?" he asked.

"Then the Lord provides," I said, repeating the wisdom of Red Smith.

"Me, too," he said again. And we both got a good laugh at the similarity of our experiences—two guys who made a living with our pens, his for drawing, mine for scribbling. Forget that he earned something like thirty million dollars a year, while the total tonnage of my income of my entire lifetime would be a fraction of just one of his years. That day we were a couple of pens for hire talking about our bad sleeping habits.

As we talked it became clear Schulz and I were similar in another way. It wasn't just having to meet deadlines. It was the anxiety, the insecurity we shared. And I was kind of amazed, really. If anything, he seemed more nervous about the whole thing than I did. I wanted to reassure him, say something like, "Sparky, you really are the all-time greatest in your line of work. You never will run out of ideas." But who was I to reassure that superstar?

So instead we talked about his drawing hand, which wasn't as steady as it used to be. He picked up a fork to show how he held his pen. He propped one hand on another, and his drawing hand grew steady. He seemed pleased with that.

Then he told me about his reading habits. He said he was always reading three or four books at the same time, but in an interesting way. "I leave books near several chairs in my house," he told me. "Whenever I sit down, I pick up a book and start reading."

Later, after we had toured the ice arena and discussed the Snoopy Tournament, he took me to the Snoopy Gallery and Gift Shop and showed me around. He seemed proud, as he should have been. He'd created an entire world in his comic strip, maybe the most recognizable world any American artist created in the twentieth century.

"I want to ask you a question," he said. "Why don't they give a Pulitzer Prize for comic strips?"

I was stumped on that one, mostly because I had no idea they didn't award one. Schulz waited for my answer. I could see this omission by the Pulitzer Committee upset him. And I wanted to make him feel better. I really did. So I said, "You know what, Sparky, you're too good for the Pulitzer Prize."

That seemed to cheer him up. He walked me to my car. He said he'd enjoyed the time we spent together. Then he said, "My wife and I would like to have dinner with you and your wife."

I assured him I would phone. And I meant it, too. But deadlines and life got in the way, and I put it off. And now I have something to regret.

45

THE LAST RIDE:
BOBB McKITTRICK
IGNORES BILL WALSH

FOOTBALL COACH FRED VONAPPEN was temporarily out of a job. He had coached at University of Hawaii, but that was over. And he had coached under Bill Walsh with the 49ers when the 49ers won Super Bowls.

In the summer of 1999, he visited NFL training camps to stay current, keep himself in the game. First, he went to Napa where the Raiders worked out. VonAppen and Raiders coach Jon Gruden were friends from 1991, when they both coached at University of Pittsburgh where vonAppen was assistant head coach. Gruden got vonAppen a place to stay at the Raiders hotel and invited him into coaches' meetings and they watched film together. Two old friends bonding over the basics of football.

At practice one day, vonAppen knelt down to get a better, more professional look at the line play. He felt a hand on his shoulder. He looked up at a Raiders intern. "Mr. Davis doesn't allow anybody to kneel on the field," the intern timidly informed vonAppen. VonAppen stood up and remembered once again how the Raiders worked. Mr. Davis—as in Al Davis—controlled everything from the big stuff to buying paper clips. Davis wasn't even on the premises that day but vonAppen felt the long reach of his arm.

After a few days with the Raiders, vonAppen drove to Stockton where the 49ers held preseason camp. Steve Mariucci was the coach in those days and Bill Walsh had returned as general manager. Walsh was vonAppen's mentor and guiding angel. Walsh invited vonAppen to Stockton to watch practice and to hang around with him. Walsh was loyal to 49ers from the glory days, and after coaching at the 49ers, vonAppen had been Walsh's defensive coordinator at Stanford during Walsh's second tenure there. To the end of his days, Walsh wanted vonAppen to like him. And vonAppen did.

There was also something else in it for vonAppen.

Someone else.

Bobb McKittrick.

McKittrick was the 49ers offensive line coach, but he wasn't just any offensive line coach. He was one of four coaches who went all the way with the 49ers, participated in all five Super Bowl wins, was integral to the dynasty. It was McKittrick, George Seifert, Ray Rhodes, and Bill McPherson.

McKittrick worked with undersized but quick, attacking offensive linemen. In all his 49ers years, he had only one first-round draft pick. He didn't care. Many line coaches are rigid and insist players do things one way. Not McKittrick. He was a teacher. He didn't care about the niceties of technique, which foot to lead with coming out of the stance, that sort of thing. As long as his linemen got where they were supposed to go, McKittrick was satisfied.

He was an ex-marine who shaved his head and wore short-sleeve shirts even in the coldest weather. He figured his players were toughing it out in the winter in Green Bay or Detroit or Buffalo and he should tough it out with them. He was a throwback guy. Walsh considered the short sleeves too macho for his taste. McKittrick thought Walsh ran like a girl. McKittrick never networked with coaches from other teams trying to find another job. He was devoted to the 49ers. He never swore and he drove a beat-up VW and was unpretentious and worked diligently on his family tree. He was incomparable at finding premier offensive linemen no one had heard of like Jesse Sapolu from Hawaii or Guy McIntyre who had been a tight end at University of Georgia. VonAppen considered McKittrick "an uncoach-like coach." VonAppen loved McKittrick and sought his approval.

Walsh and McKittrick did not like each other. Walsh considered McKittrick blunt and socially unsophisticated. McKittrick considered Walsh overly nuanced, too complicated, and political. But they needed each other and worked brilliantly together. Walsh created the passing game—among the most elegant in NFL history. McKittrick wrote the running plays, the ground game. McKittrick grounded the dreamy, creative Bill Walsh in the hard grunts and hits of football.

Walsh had capable technicians on offense, notable coaches like Sam Wyche, Mike Holmgren, Dennis Green, and Paul Hackett, but they never stepped before the entire offense when Walsh was diagramming the pass plays for the upcoming game, sometimes more than two hundred plays. The installation of the offense took place in the evening and it was Walsh's show except when it came to the running game. Then Walsh stepped aside and McKittrick diagrammed those plays. McKittrick was the only coach besides Walsh allowed at the board.

So, vonAppen, out of a job, visited 49ers training camp in 1999, and McKittrick said, "Stay by me." McKittrick was a father figure to vonAppen. This vonAppen told me. McKittrick had only a year to live. He was suffering from bile-duct cancer and there would be no cure and McKittrick, head high, posture perfect, stoically marched toward his end.

The practices were two and a half hours and they exhausted McKittrick. He had to ride a golf cart from drill to drill. After one drill, McKittrick drove over to vonAppen who watched from the sideline. "The next drill is all the way over on the other end," McKittrick told vonAppen. "Ride with me."

VonAppen didn't move. Walsh was at the practice and Walsh did not want outsiders on the practice field. VonAppen was acutely aware of being an outsider. "I can't do that," vonAppen told McKittrick. "Bill will have a shit fit if he sees me riding around in a cart."

"Screw him," the great Bobb McKittrick replied. "I'm dying of cancer. He knows that. What's he going to say to me?"

Walsh didn't say a thing and McKittrick and vonAppen took one last ride.

46

HALLOWED GROUND:
9/11, A MONTH LATER

I GET WITHIN TWO BLOCKS OF THE HORROR. I'm in New York to cover the League Division Series between the Yankees and Oakland A's. I take the subway downtown from my hotel, exit at Wall Street, and walk upstairs. When I hit the street, my senses are immediately assaulted.

First, of course, is the visual shock, the ancillary results of what those people did on September 11, almost one month to the day before I arrive. Concrete barriers block me from getting too close to the actual destruction. Looming over the barricades are miles of chain-link fences closing off the forbidden zone. Neatly placed into the holes of the fences—as a form of remembrance, as a reminder of our humanity—I see fresh bouquets. Passersby can't actually place the flowers into the fence. The hundreds of cops and National Guardsmen and women dressed in their camouflage uniforms will stop them in a heartbeat. So people call out and cajole and hope someone from the National Guard will notice them, take the bouquet, and place it.

In addition to the initial visual shock—and I'm not yet talking about actually seeing it—is the smell. It's something I've never experienced. It comes and goes, depending on the wind. Sometimes it's as sweet as burned plastic. Other times it's sour and foul and burns the insides of my nose. God knows what forms of matter contribute to the smell—atomized glass, concrete, insulation, and human remains.

In the middle of all this destruction, people who work in those old, narrow, crooked streets of Lower Manhattan are busy, rushing here and there. One woman carries a cup of designer coffee. Another wears a gas mask. Gas masks everywhere. It is inconceivable.

I walk a few blocks along with others who've come to see, remembering how my father, who worked down here, used to hold my hand as we walked along Liberty Street, Maiden Lane, Rector Street. This has become a daily pilgrimage for people from all over the world.

Many have cameras, but the police don't allow them to take photos. It's a crime scene, not to mention a war zone and a graveyard, and photos are forbidden. It's hallowed ground and it's considered a desecration to take snapshots. People do it anyway. Not because they're insensitive. They're in awe.

And then the end of the world heaves into view. I stare down one street, past the cops demanding the ID of anyone who works there, past the fence, past the dust still covering everything, and I see the abbreviated steel skeleton of one tower. It stands like a relic from an ancient civilization, except that it still smolders. Next to it lies the other mangled tower, compacted the way they crush cars in a wrecking yard. A backhoe moves back and forth on top of a gray heap collecting rubble. Four huge cranes, like giant lizards, labor nearby. A procession of trucks drives out of ground zero, their beds filled with lifeless rubble. The rubble steams—gas and smoke rolling into the air.

Nearby buildings have sides gashed from the blast, and all their windows are gone as if careless kids smashed them with rocks. A man in a black overcoat stands next to me. "I had to see this," he says softly. He'd worked across the street from the horror, he'd attended a meeting in the towers. "Now all those people are gone," he says.

He tells me about a friend who lived in Battery Park City, a group of apartment buildings two blocks from the Twin Towers. Everyone had to evacuate Battery Park City, but the authorities let his friend return to gather clothes. She walked onto her balcony, and what she saw on the floor in front of her was a hand and some fingers.

Across the street from where I stand is a parking garage. The yellow neon arrow pointing to the entrance still flashes, even though no cars enter or leave. It is one of life's absurdities. Inside the garage, I see a red sports car and other cars. And then I realize why those cars are still there and never will be claimed by their owners.

On lower Broadway, people have posted signs. One woman from Louisiana seeks information about her forty-year-old son, missing. Someone has posted a handwritten card from Luke, a first grader at Silver Oak Elementary School in San Jose, California. "I hope you will live for the rest of your life," he's written.

I hope we all live for the rest of our lives.

THE TOUGHEST GUY
IN SPORTS

T HE TOUGHEST GUYS I EVER MET were in the press box. Sure, I covered
brain-knocking boxers Mike Tyson, George Foreman, and Thomas
Hearns, and tear-your-head-off football players Fred Dean, Justin
"The Cowboy" Smith, and Patrick Willis. Compared to my press-box pals,
those guys were marshmallows.

Not everyone in a press box is tough. Some are wimps—me included. But
a particular fauna exists in the press box. I call this life-form Press Box Tough
Guys. And they scare the shit out of me. Out of everyone.

Take a Raiders game as an example. Say they aren't playing well today. Say
the coach—maybe Dennis Allen once upon a time—has made crummy play
calls and the Raiders are getting murdered. The Press Box Tough Guy begins a
loud monologue, meant for other sports writers.

"What kind of shit is this?" The voice rising to a crescendo. The voice taking over the press box. "A Little League team plays better than this. Fuck. Wait till I get to the postgame press conference. Ahma rip Dennis a new asshole. Won't know what hit him. Put the motherfucker on the spot. Rip the roof offa Oakland. Shit."

The Press Box Tough Guy is so impressive. You're in a foxhole—not sure why you're in a foxhole—but you want him on your side in a foxhole.

Raiders lose. Afterward comes the postgame presser. Everyone asking Dennis Allen questions in the gray, dank, dreary interview room at the Oakland Coliseum. Press Box Tough Guy is quiet. Waiting in the weeds, a sniper. Deadly. Finally, he speaks. You tense up. Incoming flak.

But the voice is different now. Like one of those silent-movie stars who didn't translate to the talkies. The Press Box Tough Guy is almost whispering, his tone ingratiating. Submissive. Call it kiss-ass. Wants the coach to like him. Approve of him. Be his pal. Calls the coach "Coach." A title. Wouldn't dare use the coach's name. Dennis. Afraid of being impolite.

In the press box, the Press Box Tough Guy makes fun of Raiders owner Al Davis. "Al's lost it. I'm telling you, Al's fucking lost it. What a fraud. I get a chance, ahma rip Al a new asshole."

But at an Al Davis presser—and there were many—the Press Box Tough Guy doesn't call Al "Al." The Tough Guy calls him "Mr. Davis" in a tone you'd use to address the president, a plea for approval and forgiveness if, God forbid, he offended Al Davis. Or fell out of favor. And when Al Davis answers—a throwaway answer—the Press Box Tough Guy nods his head vigorously to show he understands and feels privileged to be recognized. I call this the Graduate Student Nod.

I admire the Press Box Tough Guy, I really do. He is king of the jungle in his natural habitat—the press box. Go up there. Check him out. He'll rip you a new asshole.

48

THE REAL:
THE UNAPPRECIATED
VIRTUES OF BOXING

THEY FIND OUT YOU'RE A SPORTS WRITER, they ask, "What's your favorite sport?" Happens all the time. They're expecting some paean to baseball, football, or basketball. They want to agree or disagree, tell you why, make you listen. When I say boxing, they stare at me. *Is this guy nuts?* A friend from decades ago at Stanford, a PhD student in civil engineering from Greece, told me I wasn't a gentleman because I liked boxing.

I defend boxing, although it seems odd to defend boxing now. It has been remaindered, exists on the edge of sports as a cobwebbed memory from a former time. But from 1944 to 1964, boxing fans could watch the Friday Night Fights on television—although at the end, the fights weren't always on Friday and viewership fell. When the Friday fights went off the air, they were the longest-running program in the history of television. I loved boxing then and still love it, watch old fights on YouTube, have seen Joe Louis knock out poor Max Schmeling in the first round a hundred times.

Most sports mediate violence and aggression through a ball. In football, violent on a par with boxing, it's ball. In basketball, it's ball and basket. In tennis, it's ball, racquet, and net. In baseball, it's ball, bat, and glove. In hockey, way up there on the violence meter, it's puck, a ball variant, and net. Football, basketball, hockey, and even soccer are war games: each team tries to invade the other team's territory and put the ball (i.e., the missile, the bomb) in the opponent's net, goal, hoop (i.e., in the enemy's home, city, country).

Boxing has no balls. Its violence is direct and unmediated. Two guys wearing gloves punch each other. Simple as that. Only the most basic rules apply— compare boxing rules to encroachment in football or an offensive foul in basketball, or just about any foul in basketball, so hard to determine. In boxing, guy gets knocked down, ref counts to ten. Drama ends.

They find out you like boxing, they try to convert you. Set you on the right path, the moral path. If only they can make you understand. They are the moral do-gooders. They say boxing is brutal, people get hurt. I agree. How can you like a sport like that? I say boxers are like gladiators. They choose the sport—it's a matter of free choice. I don't tell grown people how to live or what values to embrace. Not my business.

I say people get hurt in other sports—getting hurt is not exclusive to boxing. So-called humane sports produce more hurt and death than boxing. About five hundred have died in a ring or because of boxing injuries since the adoption of the Marquess of Queensberry rules in 1884. Five hundred is too many but it's nothing compared to people who died swimming or riding bikes.

From 2005 to 2014, an average of 3,536 people drowned in the United States each year. About ten each day. If you include boat-related deaths, add 332 annually.

In 2016 alone, 814 died in the United States in bicycle-related accidents. In 2013, forty-eight thousand suffered injuries riding bikes.

I ask do-gooders if they ever considered banning swimming or bike riding, worse than boxing for sheer carnage and tragedy. They shrug as if I'm a moron and move onto the next argument. It's a progression and I've been through this progression. The difference between boxing and other life-threatening sports, they lecture, is the purpose of boxing—to inflict pain.

I say football players intend to hurt opponents. Coaches teach linebackers to "run through" running backs and quarterbacks, meaning hit them with maximum hurt. I say Robert Saleh, the 49ers' defensive coordinator, uses a slogan for his defense: *extreme violence.* I don't mean to criticize Saleh, a good guy. I'm stating a fact. He made rubber wristbands for his players. The wristbands contain the printed words *extreme violence.*

I say football is more brutal than boxing. Boxing has weight classes. You fight someone your size and you fight facing each other. In football a three-hundred-pound defensive lineman with a running start can crush a stationary 215-pound quarterback from behind. Aeneas Williams hit 49ers quarterback Steve Young with a running start and ended Young's career. I say running backs often get slammed by more than one defender, get hit from all directions and end up at the bottom of the pile of bodies. Never could happen in boxing.

I say all this can lead to permanent brain damage, often does. I say football players suffer at an alarming rate from a degenerative brain disease called chronic traumatic encephalopathy (CTE), a result of multiple concussions, so common in football. NFL players were diagnosed with more concussions in 2017 than in any season since the league began sharing the data in 2012: 281 reported concussions. Previous high, 275 in 2015.

Other grim facts, and I mean grim. Former Chicago Bears player Dave Duerson committed suicide by shooting himself in the head. Researchers found CTE in his brain. Former Atlanta Falcons player Ray Easterling committed suicide and an autopsy revealed CTE. Former linebacker Junior Seau killed himself with a gunshot to the chest, apparently leaving his brain intact for study. His family sued the NFL saying his suicide was a result of constant brain trauma he suffered in games. The Seau family settled with the league for an unspecified amount in 2018. In 2015, NFL players and the league had reached a settlement giving up to four million dollars per retired player for brain trauma, but the Seaus opted out of that settlement.

I ask do-gooders why they pick on boxing when football is so dangerous. The do-gooders, often doctors who went to fine universities and rooted for the football team on chill autumn afternoons—rah rah rah—don't want to hear about this.

I say boxing is not mostly about hurting the other guy. Like every other sport, boxing is about winning. That's why most fights go to decision. If you win by knocking someone down for ten seconds, good for you. But if you jab for twelve rounds, and show "ring generalship"—a boxing term—and win on points, well, good for you, too.

Former featherweight champion Willie Pep, who died in 2006, was regarded as a strategic genius, a conceptual fighter. An intellectual in the ring. He was one of the best boxers ever. I met Pep in 1989 and asked his philosophy: "I tried to get away the easiest way I could with my job. If I could outbox a guy, I did. I didn't try to knock anybody out. I didn't try to go in and kill anybody because when you try that, then you're open for getting whacked yourself. I boxed a hundred seventy fights that went to a decision. I don't think anybody else in the world ever did that."

As the do-gooder turns away in disgust, I try to explain why I love boxing. And I do love boxing.

I say two men stand in a twenty-foot square and put it all on the line. I use the word *men* because women did not fight when I became fascinated with boxing in the mid-1950s, so I will use the masculine pronoun for auto-biographical accuracy. One man faces another with no backup, no team, no substitutes. The fighters have their gloved fists and nothing else. They exhibit bravery, pride, heroism—words from another era, an era of self-reliance. I ad-mire self-reliance, wish I had more of it.

I don't usually consider sports to be metaphors for life. Life is more complex than games, but an element of life metaphor exists in boxing and I feel it deeply. Every great fighter gets knocked down, and this included Muhammad Ali, Sugar Ray Robinson, and Rocky Marciano. Every great fighter, as proof of his greatness, pulled himself off the canvas—the floor, the gutter—cleared his head and took up the fight yet again. I have been knocked down in life more than once, and I tried to get up and move on with courage and dignity. I saw nobility in boxing even if the boxers were not intellectuals, had not read Nietzsche or Sartre or thought much about free will. I learned from them.

*****

I am in love with The Real. Define "real" how you want. To me as a boy, boxing was the realest of the real. A knockout is real. See it. Feel it. Believe it. I am not comfortable with abstractions like how we know the external world exists. Or, is there an argument proving God? Or what were Joseph Conrad's views on colonialism and how did they influence his novels?

When I watched boxing on TV with my dad all the way through high school, I saw The Real and felt grounded in life, as grounded as when my fa-ther held my hand. Later, that all changed. I learned some of The Real was not so real. What I thought I saw in the fights—honest competition—wasn't always what I actually saw. Some of the fights were fixed—a wrinkle in reality. I don't believe most of them were fixed. When Joe Louis knocked out Max Schmeling in one round at Yankee Stadium on June 22, 1938, and broke his ribs and Schmeling cried out in pain so everyone at ringside heard him, that fight, a go-to-hell to Hitler and his master-race bullshit, was real.

When Yvon Durelle hit Archie Moore with a perfect right hand to the jaw and knocked him down in the first round on December 10, 1958, in Montreal, then knocked him down twice more in the first round, flattened him, that was real. Moore grotesquely raised himself from the canvas like a man who'd been shot. Archie later told me he lost track of being in a fight, lost track of everything. His cornermen said something but they sounded like people "speaking to me over behind a hill." Archie, in danger of losing his light heavyweight title, came back and knocked out Durelle in the eleventh round. Real.

But some fights were fixed. The Mafia controlled the sport—well, had extreme influence over it. This I didn't know as a boy. I knew it by the time my dad died. In 1960, Estes Kefauver held senate hearings about corruption in boxing. After that, everyone who cared about the sport knew the truth. And this hit me hard. It was like finding out Bill Shakespeare had a ghostwriter.

The most important figure in the era of television fights was a little man no TV viewers ever saw. Frankie Carbo.

Carbo ran boxing for the Lucchese crime family and conducted his business from Madison Square Garden. He controlled many marquee fighters and some ringside officials who scored the fights, and he fixed fights so the Mob could win bets. Win big. If the violence of other sports gets mediated through a ball, the violence of boxing got mediated through Carbo.

Carbo could be charming, rarely used threats of violence when muscling in on a fighter. If the fighter refused to go along, he often found himself shut out, boycotted. Carbo could fix fights without actually fixing them. Bring along a fighter too quickly. Match him with a bigger man before he had time to recover from a previous fight.

But Carbo used force when he had to. When manager Ray Arcel refused to cut in Carbo, he found himself in a hospital with his head bashed in by a lead pipe.

Carbo had an antagonist, someone who tried to keep boxing honest, a scholarly man and a Torah scholar named Harry Markson who had been managing director of boxing at Madison Square Garden during the heyday of the Friday Night Fights. Markson was in his eighties when I met him. He lived in Red Bank, New Jersey, where I visited him at a restaurant in 1989, dead of winter.

Markson, a voice of reason, knew Carbo, knew the boxers, knew the score.

The first time Markson met Carbo he addressed him as *Mr. Carbo*. "Imagine me saying Mr. Carbo," Markson told me.

I asked Markson if he remembered a fight Carbo fixed. I'm sure he knew many fixed fights. I'm sure they still burned him up. He took his time answering, being careful. "I'll give you an instance," he finally said, meaning one and only one. "There was a fight in Miami Beach in 1958 between Kid Gavilan and Ralph 'Tiger' Jones. Jones got the decision. The matchmaker I had at the time said to me, 'I have to make that fight over again at the Garden.' I said, 'You can't make that fight again. It was a stinking fight.'"

"I think there had been a slipup," Markson told me. "Maybe they had paid only one of the officials instead of at least two because the decision went against Gavilan and I guess that's not how it was supposed to be."

Tiger Jones lost the rematch, as expected. The fight took place in Philadelphia, not Madison Square Garden. Markson kept it out of the Garden. That much he could do.

*****

After several hours with Markson, I asked for the check and we got ready to leave. I felt bad for boxing. Felt bad for Tiger Jones, whom I had met a week earlier at his home near Kennedy Airport. He was cooking a chicken dinner for his family. "I'm not a good cook," he told me, "but they ain't starving around here." I was glad the Tiger, who never got a title shot, beat Gavilan on merit when the fix wasn't in.

I walked Markson to his car in the twilight. The ground was icy. I held his elbow. I opened the car door and helped him inside. "I don't know if I was helpful," Markson said tentatively, "but I enjoyed talking about the old days." He fired up his engine, pulled away from the curb, the exhaust from his car leaving a cloud in the cold winter air. He had reacquainted me with The Real of boxing. The dirty reality, not the apparent reality I shared with my dad.

Not that it mattered. That's what I discovered as I watched Harry's taillights fade into the distance. It didn't matter that some fights were fixed. It didn't matter that Carbo was a crook. I understood that now. The Real of the fights wouldn't change for my dad and me who had watched in good faith years ago. The fights had brought us together then, and they brought us together still. We were The Real.

49

THANKS FOR THE MEMORIES: DON ZIMMER LETS ME DOWN

D ON ZIMMER ROBBED ME.
Zimmer—known as Zim or the Gerbil, with his rollicking fat cheeks—played for the Brooklyn Dodgers when I was a boy. My dad took my friend Danny and me to Ebbets Field to see the Dodgers play the Reds. Saturday, June 23, 1956. I was eleven.

Zimmer, a utility player, was subbing for Pee Wee Reese at shortstop. In the bottom of the fourth, he came to the plate and pitcher Hal Jeffcoat beaned him. A high 2–0 fastball that broke Zimmer's left cheekbone. Zimmer lay there in the batter's box dirt. The ballpark still as a cemetery. They didn't wear helmets in those days. I started to cry.

I knew Zimmer's history. Three years earlier in the minors he got beaned and was unconscious for thirteen days. And now this. My dad told me Zimmer would be okay. What did he know?

Zimmer didn't return for three months. They drilled holes in his head to relieve the pressure. Later, he became a manager and liked to deliver this line: "I can therefore truthfully state that all of those players who played for me through the years and thought I sometimes managed like I had a hole in my head were wrong. I actually had four holes in my head."

Great line. Self-deprecating Zim. Terrific sense of humor. I met him when he was Joe Torre's bench coach with the Yankees who were visiting Oakland for a Saturday day game. Zimmer was sitting in the visitor's dugout before the game and I introduced myself and we chatted. And everything went well, Zimmer a gentleman until I hesitatingly mentioned I attended the game where he got beaned.

Zimmer's friendly eyes turned to steel. "Bullshit," he said. "Bullshit."

I stared at him.

"Every time I meet someone, they tell me they were at the game," he shouted. "If I had a dollar for every person who said they were at the game I'd be a millionaire."

"But, Don, I really was there with my dad when I was a kid."

"Bullshit."

"But, Don, that game meant a lot to me."

"Bullshit."

And I thought, *This man is overreacting in the extreme.*

And I thought, *This man is being impolite.*

And I thought, *This man is robbing me of my childhood.*

And I thought, *I should just walk away.*

And I did.

FIELD OF DREAMS:
BASEBALL AND
THE AFTERLIFE

MFATHER TREATED ME to a Mets-Dodgers doubleheader in May 1962. The Dodgers had moved from Brooklyn to LA in 1958, broke my heart and lots of hearts, and now they were returning to New York for the first time. I was sixteen. We took the subway to the Polo Grounds where the Giants used to play, where the Mets would play until they got Shea Stadium in Queens.

I had never been to the Polo Grounds. It looked like a relic. Old wood and that strange, big center field. My dad bought us seats in left field, bathed in sunglow.

I need to tell you something about my father. He was legally blind. He could see enough to walk down the street and he could make out shapes on the screen in a movie theater, but he couldn't read the newspaper or books. He was a trial lawyer and, the night before a case, my brother or sister or I would read him the legal files and he would memorize them.

Okay, so my dad and I were at the Polo Grounds, and the crowd was enormous for this homecoming—55,704. It was Game 2 of the double-header, top of the sixth, and the Dodgers had Maury Wills on second and Jim Gilliam on first with no one out. Willie Davis crushed a hard liner to Elio Chacon at short. Chacon caught the liner, then threw to Charlie Neal, doubling off Wills at second base. Neal threw to Gil Hodges at first, tripling off Gilliam. Just like that. The crowd went nuts. I never heard noise like that.

When it was all over and the crowd had settled down, my father gently touched my hand and said—I never have forgotten this—"Lowelly, what just happened?"

He didn't know. He couldn't see. He saw nothing. He took me to the Polo Grounds to make me happy. And he would be happy giving me happiness. I loved my dad. I explained the Mets pulled off a triple play and he smiled. "You don't say," he said.

And I had helped him. He needed me that moment and I delivered just as I delivered years later when he was an old man visiting me in California and I held his hand crossing a busy Oakland street.

We came together in the Polo Grounds through baseball—it was the medium of our meeting. He had bequeathed to me his love of ball, a gift from his generation to mine, and now mine to my son's. Baseball continuous, always there.

Same with football and basketball and whatever sports you shared with your folks and children. Sports, a topic bonding Americans, strangers breaking the ice with, "How about those Niners?" Or, "It's about time the Giants got a good closer."

Sports, the universal glue. Sports, a secular religion with heroes and demigods and athletes we invest with our best qualities. Sports, a world filled with moral tales of right and wrong, of weak and strong. Sports, giving us the chance to rejoice and grieve.

My father died in 1988. A year later, I was in New York. One afternoon, I ducked into a movie theater to see *Field of Dreams*. Do you remember that lovely film? At the end, Kevin Costner meets his dad, long dead—his dad miraculously a young man. They had endured a fractious relationship when the father was alive, but now on this magical ball field, they play catch. A father and son communicating through throw and receive.

And I started to cry. God, did I cry. Choke-strangled sobs. Salty hot tears pouring down my face. When the movie ended, I remained in the dark theater, head down, didn't dare walk into the lobby with my wet, red face. I cried for my dad through a baseball flick. It felt so bad and so good. *Field of Dreams* brought my dad and me together after he died. My father in that dark theater holding my hand.

51

THE PHILOSOPHER KING: FLOYD PATTERSON COMFORTS SONNY LISTON

O NE DAY, I DROVE TO NEW PALTZ, NEW YORK, to meet former heavyweight champion Floyd Patterson. This was when I was interviewing boxers after my father died. Patterson won an Olympic gold medal. Before Mike Tyson, he was the youngest to win the heavyweight title, and he was the first to regain it after Ingemar Johansson knocked him out in 1959. He knocked out Johansson in a rematch. But he avoided the best contenders, and he could not take a punch to the jaw. When he finally met Sonny Liston, a great big powerful heavyweight, Patterson got knocked out twice in the first round.

There was something in Patterson that aroused my complete sympathy, even my love. Perhaps, it was the quality of his suffering. After he lost to Johansson, he wouldn't leave the house, spending months in his basement in deep depression. After Liston knocked him out, he left the arena in a false beard and mustache. For him, a loss wasn't merely a loss. He felt erased as a human being. Never have I seen an athlete suffer more deeply or publicly. If Patterson was a hero, he was Hero as Martyr.

And he was kind, unusual in his sport. If he knocked down a fighter, there he'd be trying to help him up. If he cut a man's face, he'd switch his attack to the body. In 1964, he fought Eddie Machen, who had suffered a nervous breakdown. When Patterson felt sure he would win, he eased up on Machen. "I looked in his face," Patterson told *Sports Illustrated*, "and all I could see was the look of hurt and defeat. What would be the point in hurting him more? Would it have made me a bigger man to knock out a man who had been in an institution? I'm glad I didn't knock him out."

Patterson's father had been a truck driver in Brooklyn. There were eleven kids in his family and Patterson felt he didn't have the right to eat because he'd deprive the others. He used to hide all day in subway tunnels and, once, he scratched his face out of a family photo nullifying his existence. There were times Patterson, still a teenager, would be on his way to the gym and he'd fall asleep on the subway. He'd dream about boxing. When he woke up, everyone in the subway car was staring at him. Patterson, bathed in sweat, had been throwing punches in his sleep.

*****

His New Paltz home was a former chicken farm on twenty acres. He was fifty-four and looked too small for a heavyweight—he should have fought at light-heavy, 175 pounds, but the money for heavyweights was too tempting. A gray stubble mottled his handsome face. He was talkative, confessional, all there mentally. Boxers are the most talkative athletes, also the friendliest. As an adult, he had a conversion experience and became a devout Catholic.

We spent an afternoon together, Patterson in no hurry, Patterson enjoying the attention. Patterson talking about the joy of getting concussed. Seriously.

"When you get hurt and your brain smacks up against your skull, you're floating," he said. "Let me see. How can I explain this? Sometimes during a fight you get hit with a blow. Your opponent doesn't know that you're hurt, but you have that good, good feeling. Like you don't really give a damn. Everything is real good, real slow."

He smiled. He liked the memory. He loved boxing. He told me his first marriage didn't work because he loved boxing more than his wife.

He talked about Liston knocking him out twice. I asked if he still had regrets.

"If I want to change my life, which part?" he asked. "I came to the conclusion I don't want to change one thing. If I did, today might be different. I might not think how I think now. I'm happy with myself, completely satisfied. I've learned to accept life *really* the way it is. When I lost, I told myself not to be ashamed. I did my best. I was still ashamed. I ducked people. So, I finally told myself I wouldn't feel ashamed of feeling ashamed."

Hours later as I was leaving, Patterson walked me to my car. He still wanted to talk, needed to talk. What happened next was the crux of our interview, although I didn't know it at the time. He brought up the second fight between Muhammad Ali and Sonny Liston. In the first fight, Ali had taken the heavyweight title from Liston when Liston quit after six rounds, saying his shoulder hurt. Who knows? In the rematch, a notorious fight, Ali hit Liston with a meaningless right in the first round, Liston fell down, rolled around a while, and got counted out under strange circumstances. It looked like Liston took a dive and hadn't been subtle about it.

Patterson attended that fight in Lewiston, Maine. By now he was just another challenger. After the fight, Patterson told me, he lingered by the boxers' exit in the dark. When Liston appeared, Patterson quietly trailed him to the hotel and saw him enter the lobby and take the elevator to his room. Patterson waited. Then he called Liston on the house phone.

Liston invited him up.

"Sonny opened the door," Patterson said. "He was alone. I thought his handlers would be there, but they weren't. I went up there to let him know I went through the same thing when he beat me. He was a big brute of a man, but he could not look me in my face. He kept turning away. He would look at me for a second and then he would look down. Maybe he was embarrassed. I would have loved to know what was going through his mind."

"I wonder if Liston threw that fight," I said.

"I've thought that, too," Patterson said. "Clay was not a puncher. [Patterson refused to use the name Ali.] I know because I fought him twice. I saw Cleveland Williams hit Liston with everything and Liston just walked through it. [Cleveland Williams was the hardest puncher in that era of heavyweights.] When Clay knocked Liston out, he threw a punch almost like a push. Then Liston rolled around on the canvas. I found it hard to believe. I stayed with Sonny about half an hour. He didn't add much to the conversation. After a while, I started running out of words. It's hard to keep a conversation going when one guy isn't talking. So I left."

*****

When I returned to California, I talked about Patterson and Liston with the chairman of the Department of French and Italian at Stanford, a Frenchman named Alphonse Juilland, a former professor of mine whom I called Prof. He was twenty-three years older than I, and he was a mentor and father to me on the West Coast—and I needed a mentor/father in those days. And he was a boxing fan. Just like me. He had watched the same television fights I watched with my dad, at the same time I watched them with my dad. The Prof and I constantly talked about fighters from the past as if they were current and young.

The Prof heard me out, said the story about Patterson and Liston was fascinating. "First, look at the story from Liston's point of view," he said. "A few hours earlier, he had been the focal point of the world. Millions of people watched that fight. And then he was alone, cast off, discarded, without even his handlers in his room.

"Patterson is very complex. He created the scene. It was like a little drama he wrote. I think of him furtively following Sonny through the dark streets, calling him from the lobby: 'Hello, Sonny. It's Floyd. May I come up?' And Sonny accepting because everyone else had left him.

"And what did Patterson get out of it? Sure, he went because he's a nice guy, because he's the only one who really could have empathy for Sonny. He also went, I think, to see Liston, the man who'd brought him down, now brought down himself. That's obvious. But don't you think there is something else?"

"Something else?" I repeated.

"Yes, there is something else," the Prof said. "By going there to be kind to the man who ruined him, Patterson was also forgiving himself for being knocked out twice in the first round by Sonny. It was a moment of absolution for both of them."

Rest in Peace, Floyd Patterson: 1935–2006.

52

SONNY LISTON
SIGNS HIS NAME

"**Y**OU'RE TO BE IN BED BY TEN, YOUNG MAN," my mother warned as she and my father left the house. *Not on your life*, I thought. It was a Friday night in the winter of 1956, and I was eleven years old. My parents had made the fatal error of leaving me in charge of my little sister—but no one in charge of me. Shortly before ten, my sister safely tucked in bed, I went to the living room, where my parents had a huge overstuffed couch that sighed a weary whoosh every time I sat on its cushions. I arranged throw pillows around its perimeter and sprawled in luxury. The idea of staying up past bedtime made me tingle with sinful delight.

Across from the couch stood an enormous DuMont console television, a giant mahogany square that looked like a hunk of dark chocolate with a screen sunk in its middle. At ten o'clock sharp, I turned on the TV and began to flip through the channels. As the dial came to rest on channel four, my attention was seized by the emphatic rhythms of marching music. "To look sharp every time you shave," a voice sang, "to feel sharp and be on the ball." Then the announcer proclaimed, "The Gillette Cavalcade of Sports is on the air."

I sank into the couch—whoosh. I had never seen a professional fight before and waited for the start with the thrill and fear of someone attending a forbidden rite. The boxers were lightweight contenders Baby Vasquez and Paolo Rosi.

Rosi, I learned as I watched, was a bleeder. Next to having a glass jaw, being a bleeder is the most tragic affliction in boxing. I thought Rosi outfought Vasquez, but all the blood flowing from Rosi's face forced the referee to halt the fight in the seventh round. It did not seem fair that Rosi lost. Long after the bout was over, I lingered on the couch trying to find an answer to what I'd seen. I dimly understood that boxing offers no guarantee of justice. A fight is a sad, stark, compact little drama—and that made it endlessly fascinating to me. By the time I slipped into bed that night, I was hooked.

For the next six years, I was consumed by boxing. On Monday, Wednesday, and Friday nights—my mother's 10:00 P.M. bedtime quickly disappeared in the face of my passion—I would go to the living room to sit in front of a television set peopled with the fighters of the '50s. But fighters for me were two-dimensional silhouettes who waged war in a miniature black-and-white world.

I did not attend my first professional fight until 1962. Dick Tiger, soon to be the middleweight champion, was taking on Henry Hank, a ferocious puncher who never bothered to learn the finer points of the jab and defense. I rode up to the old Madison Square Garden on the subway, visions of smoky arenas bobbing and weaving in my mind. I was sixteen and fervently romantic. Tonight would be the real thing. I arrived two hours early and bought a ringside seat. The Garden was nearly deserted.

That first fight was decidedly anticlimactic. Tiger walked all over Hank, who waited in vain to deliver the big blow. At the end, Hank seemed grateful to be alive. The audience applauded politely, as if at a cricket match.

I left the Garden bored; I hadn't missed very much in all those years of watching the Friday Night Fights on that ancient twenty-inch television. As my eyes adjusted to the dark of Eighth Avenue, I saw a large black man in a worn gray overcoat standing alone. He looked old. But after a few moments, his shape resolved itself into that of Sonny Liston, the first-ranked heavyweight challenger in the world for Floyd Patterson's heavyweight title. I went up to him and said a tentative hello. He smiled at me, so I took out my program and asked for his autograph. Writing, as I was about to find out, was not one of Sonny's stronger points.

Liston took his right hand out of his pocket. The very sight of it was dazzling. It was enormous. A large gold ring and a watch with a gold expansion band glittered against his skin. Sonny produced an expensive-looking pen that looked like a gold toothpick in his fingers and started writing. In what must have required greater effort than defeating heavyweight contenders Zora Folley, Eddie Machen, and Wayne Bethea, he struggled through a capital C. When completed, his *Charles* looked like the innocent scrawl of a child. Then he punctiliously put down a set of quotation marks, which must have looked to him as exotic as hieroglyphics, and tried a capital *S*. Suddenly he stopped and mentally paced around it the way Picasso might have pondered a troublesome brushstroke. A low rumble of disapproval issued from his throat; he scratched out the *S* and started all over again.

After a painfully long time, he mastered *Charles "Sonny" Liston*, looked up as pleased as if he had completed a work of art, and handed me the program. By this time a crowd had gathered; all had programs and all demanded autographs. Sonny patiently submitted to the signing ceremony until someone abruptly broke the silence. "What's gonna happen when you fight Patterson?"

Liston looked up and the faint smile vanished from his face. He answered matter-of-factly, as though telling the time. "I'll knock him out in the first round," he decreed, and went back to the signing. I began to drift off toward the subway while I considered what he'd said about beating the heavyweight champ. After a few moments, I reached the conclusion that Sonny Liston might know how to sign his name, but he sure didn't know anything about boxing.

53

THE KILLER: SUGAR RAY ROBINSON'S GRIEF

I HAVE BEEN A COLLECTOR of the voices of great boxing champions. I have recorded Muhammad Ali, Carmen Basilio, Ray Leonard, George Foreman, Ken Norton, Floyd Patterson, Archie Moore, and others.

In 1989, when Sugar Ray Robinson died, I went to my basement and searched for his tape. It is the most precious in my collection. I listened to it in the silence of my study, straining to hear his voice because the tape was old and his voice had become faded and marred by static. He held the welterweight and middleweight titles and defined a generation of boxing from 1940 into the 1960s.

I had gone to see him one bright morning in 1980 at the Sugar Ray Robinson Youth Foundation in Los Angeles. When I got there, the secretary said Ray would arrive soon, but it was almost an hour before he showed up, unshaven and apologetic. He called me "Old Buddy." We went into his office, but before I could begin the interview, an executive from the foundation walked in and sat down in a chair. As I recall, his name was Shelly.

I wondered why someone had to monitor what we said. I looked at Ray. He was in his late fifties, his face still spectacularly handsome. I saw scars near his eyes, the road map of his profession, a clue to his curriculum vitae. He had led a glamorous life, winning and losing several fortunes, and he had traveled with a large entourage as if he were a king. But that morning, the fire had gone out of him.

He spoke softly while Shelly listened. He told us he had lived down the street from Joe Louis in Detroit and, as a boy, would carry Joe's bag to the Brewster Gym. He would go away to training camp with Joe later on.

"I used to be in camp with him and old Jack Blackburn, a great trainer," Ray said. "At night, Jack would get us around the fire and talk to Joe and me about the art of self-defense. He told me this left hand is offense. [Ray held up his legendary left and balled it into a fist.] This right hand is defense. You only need one hand to protect yourself. A man can't throw but one punch at a time. [Ray swatted away an imaginary blow with his right hand.]"

Shelly sat quietly. With no prompting, Ray changed the subject to his fight against Jimmy Doyle in 1947.

"A couple of nights before the fight with Jimmy Doyle, I dreamed I knocked him out and he died," Ray said sadly. "I got up and told the commission I didn't want to fight because I believed in my dreams. They said, 'Oh, Sugar, you've got to go in there and try to win this fight.'

"Every time I close my eyes, I see that fight. I almost went out of my mind. Because the funny thing is, I dreamed this the night before it happened. I dreamed I knocked him out and he died. I got up and told the commission I didn't want to fight because I believed in my dreams. They said, 'Oh, Sugar, you've got to go in there and try to win this fight.'"

Shelly sighed and stared at the floor when Ray told the story the second time.

Robinson beat Doyle to death. A priest and a minister had convinced him to go through with the fight even though, as Ray told me, "Sugar's dreams come true."

Doyle had taken the fight to buy a house for his mother. Robinson bought her the house. At a coroner's inquest, Robinson was asked if he knew Doyle was in trouble, and Robinson famously replied, "It's my business to keep fighters in trouble."

Ray briefly told me about fighting Gene Fullmer and Basilio and Rocky Graziano. But, as if his mind contained only one topic, one groove, he narrated the Doyle story a third time from start to finish. Shelly politely ended the interview.

"It was nice to meet you, Old Buddy," Ray told me.

Ray's obituary said he suffered from Alzheimer's disease, more likely dementia pugilistica from head trauma. I was witnessing the early stages of his illness and Shelly was there, I'm sure, to make certain Ray didn't say anything to embarrass the foundation.

What impresses me is how Ray was torturing himself thirty-three years after the fight. This had been the defining incident of his life. He had been the greatest fighter who ever lived, but as his mind slowly sank into forgetfulness, he could not permit himself to forget one horrifying fact: he killed a man.

54

THE *NOT*: WHAT MAKES GOOD SPORTS WRITING

I HAVE SPENT DECADES THINKING ABOUT WRITING. When people ask what I like best about my job, I say the writing. They are always disappointed, want me to say I'm in love with sports. I *am* in love with sports, but I love writing more. I could write about a glass of water if it came to that.

I have thought long about writing sports columns, because I have written thousands, and because a sports column is a genre and an art form. A humble art form but an art form nonetheless practiced by serious writers—Ring Lardner, Red Smith, Jim Murray. Writing sports columns is about giving an opinion, but it's more than that. Sports columns are heavily featurized. They bring famous people to life in words. Unlike editorials, sports columns give pictures and sounds. A good sports column gets into things fast, in the first sentence, and builds tension and suspense, and leads to a boffo ending. Nails it. All in eight hundred words, sometimes a few more.

Writing sports columns means using American prose: declarative, active sentences with few dependent clauses; no passive voice; hardly any adverbs. It means hearing in your head Elmore Leonard or Donald E. Westlake or even Bernard Malamud, not William Faulkner or Virginia Woolf, God forbid.

It means having faith. Even if you don't know where you're going, you will find your way as you write. Not by thinking or even planning. By writing. You will find your ending when you reach the end—that's what endings are for.

I have asked myself this. What is my writing about? It seems like a simple question with a simple answer. It's not. A column surely can be about starting an argument. The Giants need a new third baseman. Something like that. Or it can be a character study—to show what Joe Montana really is like. Those are elements of sports writing. But isn't there more? Isn't there more to all writing than the essential theme—or what someone perceives as the theme?

Joseph Conrad, a confirmed pessimist, once wrote he could tell the whole history of mankind on a cigarette paper: "They were born, they suffered, they died." Meaning life's truths are limited, repetitive, standard. We live them. We know them.

What matters to a writer is the writing itself. The doing—how a writer writes about the standard themes.

In column-writing, this means things I tried for and missed so many times. It means the style, the syntax, the rhythm of the prose. It means personality and tone. It means wit or pathos or anger or lyrical softness. It means writing with anger or love or penetrating analysis. It means bringing something new and unexpected. It means leading to an ending that makes a reader think or makes a reader happy or sad or angry. Makes a reader do something besides move mechanically to the next article.

It means telling a story, calling a character to life, engaging a reader's emotions. Going for the emotions when going for the brain—presenting an intelligent argument—isn't sufficient.

Early in 2018, former 49er Dwight Clark organized a lunch for eight sports writers in the small town of Capitola, California, near Santa Cruz. Clark had been diagnosed with ALS—Lou Gehrig's Disease—and he had trouble walking, used a motorized wheelchair, and was beginning to lose speech. This handsome, forever-young athletic man who made The Catch in 1982, ushering in the 49ers dynasty.

It was an hour-and-a-half drive from the Bay Area to Capitola, but we made it, all of us, because we cared for Dwight Clark. He endured through the meal—and I mean endured—and after a while he was tired and needed to go home. Before we split up, I said we should make the Dwight Clark Media Lunch an annual, and he agreed and everyone else agreed. An annual.

I wrote a column about the lunch and ended with the words, "yes, yes, yes, yes, yes." It was not a thought. It was a purely emotional appeal that Dwight would be okay in a year. Yes. Okay enough to host another lunch. Yes. A lunch that we would attend. Yes. It was a plea and a prayer and a cry from the heart. A prayer denied because he died a few months later.

And I have thought about this. Most of all—and this is the rock-bottom truth—writing a column, writing anything, means the writer is not allowed to be boring. Not for a single paragraph or sentence or clause. Not even for a word. How a writer achieves this *not* is the writer's primary business and challenge and joy. Writing lives on the *not*.

55

HIS NIBS AND THE BURRITO: FABULOUS SPORTS HEADLINES

D AVE NEWHOUSE said the greatest newspaper headline he ever saw was about Nibs Price. By *greatest*, he meant laugh riot, one of those brilliant mistakes that makes the pursuit of journalism wonderful.

We called ourselves the Hacks, a group of old sports columnists, mostly retired. We met irregularly to reminisce and lie to each other. A West Coast version of the opening scene in *Broadway Danny Rose*. Mitch Juricich was our leader, a golf writer and commentator on the TV show *Hooked on Golf*.

This time we met at TPC Harding Park golf course in San Francisco, in the big dining room. After we had ordered, Newhouse, now retired from the *Oakland Tribune*, talked about the headline for the obit of Clarence Merle "Nibs" Price, who had been head basketball and football coach at the University of California in Berkeley, coached there thirty-six years. Price died on a Saturday in 1968 and, because he was local and famous, the *Oakland*

Tribune rushed to produce an article for its late edition.

Newhouse was giving the background, and everyone else at the table chuckled—Art Spander, Mark Purdy, Scott Ostler, Juricich. They knew where this was going. I didn't, a gap in my education.

"You really never heard this story?" Ostler said to me, as if I'd spent my life under a rock.

I shook my head.

"They were in a real hurry," Newhouse said about the people putting together the Nibs article. Newhouse explained they had to remake the front page of the sports section, remake it fast. One reporter wrote the copy and another went in search of a mug shot.

"You have to understand we used zinc plates in those days," Newhouse said.

This was the key to the story, but Newhouse saw my blank face.

"It was before computers," Newhouse said. "It was the metal-type days. They found the photo but they couldn't see the image because it was smeared with ink from use—that's what happened to zinc plates."

An *Oakland Tribune* writer, Pat Frizzell, came up with the headline, Newhouse said. Frizzell liked grand headlines with a metaphysical theme like "Baseball Player Goes to Golden Diamond in the Sky."

By now the other Hacks were laughing and coughing. "You're going to love this," Ostler told me.

"When the paper came out," Newhouse said, "everyone gazed at it in shock."

Because when they saw the photo printed from the zinc plate—finally saw it—Nibs Price, God love him, was holding a phone in his left hand. Nibs was looking up, seemingly staring at the headline, the one above his head which read: *Death Calls Nibs Price.*

"I guess Nibs took the call," Newhouse said.

*****

Then Newhouse told about the second-funniest headline in sports-headline history. I'll break away from the Hacks and explain my experience with this headline, one all the Hacks knew about except me. It involved Red Smith, the famous sports columnist who died in 1982, and it appeared in the *San Francisco Examiner*.

I drove to the San Francisco Public Library's main branch to see the headline for myself on microfilm. I live in Oakland. The Oakland Public Library main branch has microfilm of every edition of the *San Francisco Chronicle* but, for some obscure reason, it doesn't carry the *San Francisco Examiner*.

I parked at the Civic Center Garage on a bright, sunny, cool day—quintessential San Francisco—and wandered around lost because at my age, seventy-two, I didn't often drive to San Francisco. First, I walked into the Asian Art Museum, realized this wasn't the library, then finally found the right place, which I entered from street level. I went down a steep staircase to a main lobby with doors and signs all over the place. It was different from Oakland Public, a place for a few readers and researchers and the homeless who spend the day there and use the bathrooms. San Francisco Public also was a refuge for the homeless, but it was busy with serious library people hustling here and there, entering and exiting rooms, their faces focused and purposeful. It reminded me of the busy, crowded Fulton Street subway station in Manhattan. Alive with all that life.

I took the elevator to the fifth floor and asked for the microfilm room, but it wasn't like the microfilm room in Oakland, which was simple and resonated 1950s. For this one, you needed to get a computer in sync with the microfilm machine. When I asked the attendant, a young man, for help, he looked at me like I had suggested sex. So, I struggled for forty-five minutes to figure out the thing and found the news story about the death of Red Smith. But the headline was ordinary, pedestrian, something about "well-known columnist dies," and I wondered what Newhouse and the Hacks had gone on about.

I began to leave the library defeated. Took the elevator to the ground floor below street level and wearily climbed the high flight of stairs to the street and began walking to the garage. Tired. Worn out. But I stopped. It was my Come-to-Jesus moment. I told myself, for heaven's sake, I was a journalist—used to be—and I was in San Francisco, a great city of the world, and I was running away.

Stay, I told myself. *Enjoy yourself.*

I walked across the plaza toward city hall, the sun speckled on the ground, and saw in the distance food trucks—Mexican, Vietnamese, Chinese, hot dogs, you name it. And people were standing in line waiting to order and talking and laughing. San Francisco is the most playful city. What the hell, I bought a burrito. I had flopped on Red Smith, but I still could have a San Francisco experience.

The burrito tasted good. They had set up folding chairs near the food trucks. I ate the burrito sitting in a chair with the warm sun shining on my back, a lovely feeling. Reassuring. Halfway through the burrito a thought leaped across a synapse in my brain.

"There's another Red Smith story," I said out loud. "There has to be a follow-up. That's the one I'm looking for."

But did I really want to trudge back across the plaza, cross Larkin Street, walk into the Main Library/Fulton Street Station with all those people hustling in and out, and hustle down the stairs to catch an elevator upstairs?

Hell, yes, I did.

I had learned the microfilm-computer combo. I knew the exact date I was looking for. And when I got to the reading room, my spot was unoccupied. Now I was in business. I raced through the microfilm and there, the day after Red Smith died, I saw a reprint of a *New York Times* column by Dave Anderson honoring Smith. In the second paragraph, Anderson wrote of Smith his dear friend, "All he ever wanted to be was a 'newspaper stiff,' as he often identified himself."

That, apparently, was the key sentence for the headline writer. It is standard practice to take the headline from the story, shows the headline writer read and digested the material and can present it to the reader in an eye-catching way.

This headline sure was eye-catching: "The No. 1 'newspaper stiff.'" Newspaper stiff was in quotation marks to show it was a direct quote, and that was good as far as it went. But the headline, if you thought about it, definitely meant the working stiff in question was the number-one newspaper stiff in America, as in the number-one dead newsman. As in a stiff in a morgue. As in serious rigor mortis. Red Smith was a stiff newspaper stiff.

When I got the giggles in the reading room, a homeless man staring out the window looked at me with disapproval.

Number One newspaper stiff?

Well, I wanted to die at the silliness of it all. And I remembered, yet again, that although life is tragic, it is also comic. And the proof of that endless dichotomy was right there in front of me.

I silently thanked Dave Newhouse for alerting me to the stiff headline. I left the library and laughed all the way across the Bay Bridge. When I got home, I told my wife the whole story—how I almost fled San Francisco but ate a burrito, suddenly figured out the existence of a follow-up article, walked back across the plaza, looked at the microfilm, and found the fabulous headline.

"It was the burrito," my wife said.

"Huh?"

"You had low blood sugar and you ate the burrito and it helped you think straight."

"It did?"

"You think you're the hero of this story," she said, "but you're not. It's the burrito."

56

GO-KART MOZART: DALE EARNHARDT JR. FINALLY WINS A RACE

I T STARTED WITH DALE EARNHARDT JR. He was in Sonoma County promoting the upcoming NASCAR race at Infineon Raceway. My paper, the *Santa Rosa Press Democrat*, covered the race like mad because it was in our backyard. My editor asked me to attend Earnhardt's news conference and write a column previewing the race. No problem. The raceway sent out an email with something about go-karts. I didn't give it a thought.

I had houseguests at the time. I apologetically told them I'd be gone several hours covering auto racing. My guests asked to come along, wanted to meet Dale Jr., see the track, see how I worked. Sure, I said.

My guests were Eric and Doris Kimmel. Eric is a well-known children's writer. His most famous work, *Hershel and the Hanukkah Goblins*, recently reissued in a twenty-fifth anniversary edition, is the best children's Hanukkah book ever, anywhere, anyplace, and a 1990 Caldecott Honor Book, a tremendous distinction.

I frankly was surprised Eric had any interest in NASCAR. He doesn't know sports. Doesn't know the difference between the American League and National League. I doubt he's ever watched a NASCAR race, NFL game, NBA game, or any game.

Eric spends his time writing and reading fairy tales. I think his mind is populated with goblins and fairy princesses and spiders that talk. He and I grew up in Flatbush, Brooklyn, went to the same elementary school—PS 193—the same junior high school—Andries Hudde—and the same high school—Midwood. I was a year ahead of Eric and didn't meet him until college, exceedingly strange. We both attended Lafayette College in Easton, Pennsylvania, and were fraternity brothers before I went west to graduate school at Stanford to become a professor—at least, that's what I thought.

Like me, Eric has a Brooklyn mouth—something he never reveals in his writing. He is ironic, sometimes crossing the border to sarcasm, his words full of double meanings. His grandmother, who lived in his house when he grew up, spoke to Eric in Yiddish. Sometimes I feel Eric is translating from the Yiddish when we talk, his declarative sentences ending in rising inflections like interrogatives with an insinuation of doubt or skepticism. Like, "That's the real story, Lowell?"

So, he, Doris, and I drove to the raceway in the Sonoma County wine country. When we arrived, a public-relations person directed us to an area unfamiliar to me. I asked the PR person what was going on. "Dale's racing an eleven-year-old kid in go-karts."

Somehow Dale Jr. racing an eleven-year-old in a go-kart didn't strike me as strange. The raceway had pulled all kinds of stunts in the past. Once, it set driver Rusty Wallace loose in a San Francisco cab. He picked up fares and accepted tips and, only at the end of each ride, revealed who he was. All the local TV stations got video of the gag and the raceway loved it. Another time, a racer cooked spaghetti carbonara at a fancy San Francisco restaurant. And another time a racer whizzed me around the road course real fast with my lunch rising to my epiglottis so I'd have an ass-on experience of mind-blowing speed.

Eric, Doris, and I sat in temporary mini-stands along with an army of media covering the event. We looked like adults sitting in kindergarten chairs. We saw the go-karts waiting there, junior versions of racing cars. Everything was diminutive. We'd arrived at Munchkin Land and I expected the Lollipop Guild to show up for their signature number. There was something miniature-golf about the whole thing—miniature golf on wheels.

Dale Jr., as you would expect, had trouble fitting in his go-kart—I imagined them using a shoehorn to squeeze him in. The kid fit like a champ. When they started racing, there was no vroom vroom, the background noise of NASCAR that makes kidneys vibrate and tooth fillings shake, rattle, and roll. And no gasoline smell—gas fumes being the medium NASCAR drivers inhabit, like you and I inhabit a world of oxygen and nitrogen and fish inhabit water.

Dale and the kid putt-putted courteously down the minuscule straightaways, made tight turns around the tiny track. And they went around and around and around. I wrote notes in my reporter's notebook, marking down laps and lap times as if covering a real competition. Wrote visuals of Earnhardt, son of the famous Dale Sr.

After Dale Jr. kicked the kid's ass, his first win of the year, if you could call that a win, they brought everyone to an interview room, Earnhardt and the kid and the media. The racers sat on a stage, the rest of us in chairs facing them. As we sat down, I told Eric, "This is business. Don't say a word."

"I'll be good," he promised.

A representative from the speedway opened things up for questions, and the media focused on the issue at hand, go-karting. Taking the lead, I asked Dale Jr. how his vehicle handled. Was he satisfied with his performance? Was losing to his competitor ever a possibility? Dale Jr. answered dutifully, seriously, no winking at the reporters. We all copied down his words on go-karts. We also asked questions about the NASCAR race in a few weeks, but mostly we talked go-karting. We interviewed the kid at length, the kid in ecstasy to occupy a stage with Dale Jr.

When it was over, I asked Eric, "What did you think?"

I was looking for validation, for his appreciation of the journalistic process, or praise for my perceptive questions. Eric looked at me, and from somewhere deep in his past, translating Yiddish into English, he said for everyone including Dale Jr. to hear, "For *this* you went to Stanford?"

57

BARON DAVIS
LEARNS MANNERS

B ARON DAVIS WAS DRIBBLING A BASKETBALL. He wasn't supposed to be dribbling a basketball. It was Golden State Warriors Media Day 2007, just before the NBA season started, and the Warriors invited the press to interview the players. This had always been a casual, friendly get-together. At an appointed time, a player would sit at a large round table in the Warriors gym and chat with eager reporters. It's how the NFL works things during Super Bowl Week, players at tables with media.

Of course, the Warriors don't do it that way anymore. They are three-time world champs and the players come into an interview room one at a time and sit on a stage and hold press conferences with the media down below. Presidential. And that ruins the fragile thread of intimacy. So many things ruin the fragile thread of intimacy in our lives.

Davis was supposed to sit at a table already populated with reporters and columnists and TV and radio people. But Davis wasn't sitting. He was dribbling. And shooting. The table was near one of the baskets and Davis apparently thought he needed practice. He shot baseline jumpers. He drove for layups. Sometimes went behind his back and did a stutter step.

Steve Bitker, the morning sports anchor for KCBS radio, was assigned to get audio from Davis, a Warriors star, ordinarily an easy assignment. You sit. He talks. You record his words. But Davis wasn't sitting. He was doing a solo basketball performance. "Ask me questions and I'll answer," he shouted over his shoulder as he sank a jumper.

Bitker was chasing him around the court, chased Davis holding his recorder and microphone near Davis' mouth, as close as he could get, which wasn't very close. Bitker's face was full of frustration. Bitker wasn't getting any audio except for heavy breathing, his and Davis'. And I was watching this absurdist drama, which was either a fuck-you to the media—not the first time an athlete delivered a fuck-you—or maybe Davis, who had always seemed agreeable, was just clueless.

That's when my mother entered the gymnasium. My mother, Eve, a New York City elementary school teacher. She was dead by then, but she was there. I knew she was there. She had been loving but stern. Had standards. Established limits. Made us set out our school clothes the night before, my brother, my sister, and me. One time, when I was nine, I was sitting at the kitchen table doing homework, which she required—sitting there while we worked. I did a half-assed job. Ink splotches on paper. I handed the paper to her. Her face never changed. She merely ripped it in half and said, "Now do it again."

I felt my mother as I watched Davis. It was more than feeling her. It was listening to her. My mother and father still exist within me. I hear them cheering for me, criticizing me, guiding me as they always did. I hear them. My mother would have disapproved of Baron Davis, such bad manners, so rude to adults doing an honest job.

And as I watched poor Steve Bitker running around humiliated by Davis, I said in a loud stern voice—my mother's voice—"Baron, sit down. Sit down now."

He stopped dribbling the ball. He stared at me. He tried to take in what he'd heard—*sit down now.*

I said to him, "It's time to be a gentleman, Baron. Be a gentleman."

He set the ball on the floor, made sure it stayed put. He walked over to the table, pulled out the chair designated for him, sat in it. Looked each of us in the eye and, damn, if he didn't give the best interview he ever gave.

Thanks, Mom.

58

CHAIR: NO CURSING IN THE PRESS BOX

I NEVER TOLD ANN KILLION TO SHUT THE FUCK UP. But I thought it.

Ann is a sports columnist for the *San Francisco Chronicle*, a damned good columnist and a damned good friend. But she used to be noisy on deadline. This I could understand. It's about the anxiety of writing, something all writers who care about their work experience.

You feel anxious, scared, even nauseated on deadline if you're devoted to craft, if you aren't just putting words on a screen and going fast to Quote City, using dull quotes from the players like "We need to improve our intensity." To fill up your word count and get the misery of writing over with.

Ann cares. We would sit in the press box—I'm thinking 49ers at their new place in Santa Clara—sit in the second row at the table stretching along the football field, sit perched above the field so we could look down and see the patterns in the plays, sit at yards and yards of table with all the columnists looking at their computer screens, searching for an angle, figuring out what to write. What to fucking write.

Football is the hardest sport to translate into words. Compare football to other sports. In boxing, one guy defeats another, sometimes with a one-punch knockout, or by winning on points. It's easy to describe this one-on-one encounter.

Baseball is easy, too. Beautiful and easy. In every game, one play stands out as crucial, as defining. Or one player—often the pitcher—is defining and central to the drama. And a columnist writes about that play or that player—the ninth-inning home run by Barry Bonds. Simple as that.

Not so with football. Each team is two teams, offense and defense. Well, special teams is a third team but I never much cared about kickoffs, punts, and field goals unless, of course, the placekicker screwed up, lost the game, and I had to write one of those heartbreak-of-defeat columns, which I hated to write.

As the third quarter winds down in a football game, you sit in the press box doodling on your computer screen, trying to find a topic. Football is so various and complicated. Do you write about the quarterback, always a good fallback position because everyone wants to read about the quarterback, or do you write about the free safety who intercepted that pass in the second quarter, or the head coach whose game plan seemed Neanderthal, or the left tackle who missed a key block?

What the hell do you write about? This choice among so many options is dizzying and migraine-inducing. And after you've decided—*God, I hope I made the right choice*—you hustle down to the locker room, but the quarterback or free safety or left tackle has nothing much to say, and the coach says he has to look at the tape before he can be definitive. And you ride the elevator up to the press box, palms sweating, trying to convince yourself you have a good topic, you have an entire column, you really do. And this is where the insanity begins.

You avoid writing because you're scared shitless to start even though your deadline is in a few hours and it takes time to write, even if you're confident, know what you're doing. Instead of writing, you start talking. Talking to anyone. Talking loudly and nervously. Panic talking.

Ann would do this, especially in her early days as a columnist. And I understood. I had been there, would be there. But sometimes I had my topic and was ready to let it rip, but my head was filled with her words. Not mine.

I had made a deal with myself years before. I was as terrified as anyone writing a live column on deadline. But I refused when possible to go crazy at that moment because it was not helpful. *You can go crazy later*, I promised myself. *There's just no time now.*

Going crazy in the press box did not put words on the screen. Did not bring me closer to the end. So, I pledged myself a full-blown berserko episode later that night at home, when, jacked up on adrenaline, often with a glass of wine, I'd pace around the house talking to myself in voices that weren't even my own, getting all of that out while my wife, God love her, slept peacefully in the bedroom. This insane episode was simply a pleasure deferred, an indulgence I could not allow myself in the press box where, holding my nose, I would dive off the high board, do a Triple Lindy, and land headfirst in the deep end. And write my ass off.

And when I wrote, my fingers moving as fast as I was thinking, the words pouring out, a strange thought would occur to me. It was about James Joyce. I knew I never could write like that genius. Never in a million years. And although I felt jealous about the unfairness of life, Joyce having all the talent instead of me, I could cheer myself up. Did cheer myself up. Would imagine myself leading Joyce into the press box at a Niners game and telling him, "Jimmy, you have three hours to write a thousand words on this game."

Telling this to James Joyce who took seven years to write *Ulysses*. I could imagine Joyce stumped, not able to write fifteen words in the three hours, worrying endlessly about the placement of a comma. I could imagine I was doing speed writing Joyce couldn't handle if his life depended on it. I could imagine the great Joyce talking loudly, bullshitting just to avoid the moment of putting fingers on keys. And it made me feel great, made me feel less crazy, comforted me, helped me get started.

Eat your heart out, Jimmy.

Which brings me back to Ann Killion. I understood her prewriting talking. Had complete empathy for her. But she was in the way. "You're taking the fall," Bogart said to Mary Astor. And one day on deadline, I motioned to Ann, and we walked away from the other writers, Ann's eyes filled with questions.

"I would never say to you, 'shut the fuck up,'" I told Ann, "even though I wouldn't hesitate saying it to male writers."

"I hope you wouldn't say it to me," she said.

"But when you're noisy I need to say something out of self-preservation."

She looked sad.

"Here's what I'm going to do. When you're talking loud on deadline and I can't concentrate on my writing, I will look over at you and say, 'chair.'"

"Chair?" she said.

"Yes, chair. Chair is a code word. Chair means shut the fuck up, but when I say chair, no one will know what I mean. It's just between us."

Ann smiled.

"That's fair," she said. "That's a good idea."

And she walked away laughing. I heard her say "chair" and I heard her giggle.

Over the years if I felt she was loud on deadline, I would call out—in a gentle voice—"Ann, chair." And she would say, "Yes, yes, chair. I get it." And she would quiet down and write.

And there it stood until after one 49ers game a few years ago. I was having trouble writing, trouble getting into the column. And I was talking to somebody, talking to anybody, talking loudly, avoiding the horrible moment of truth. People were looking at me angrily. I had no power to stop myself. I was the noisy offender. Ann stood up, stared at me like a teacher confronting a problem child.

"Am I going to have to chair you?" she asked in a firm voice, making a noun into a verb.

I thought about what Ann said. She never actually chaired me. She merely expressed the threat of chair. Even in code she was polite to the max. But I got the point and I did the right thing. I shut the fuck up.

59

APOSTROPHE *S*

I N BOOKS, they always put in the second *S* for possessives: *Barry Bonds's piping-hot slice of pepperoni pizza with extra cheese.* In newspapers, my world, we leave out the second *S*: *Barry Bonds' piping-hot slice of pepperoni pizza with extra cheese.* Newspapers save space by avoiding the redundant second *S*. If I ever get this collection published, I pray my editor allows my apostrophe to speak for itself.

60

BYLINE FEVER: A SPORTS WRITER'S ADDICTION

I AM A MODEST PERSON, but I needed to see my byline. Every day if possible. I never earned lots of money—I'm a writer, for heaven's sake—but the byline compensated for not having a second home in Tahoe or for driving a Prius instead of a Mercedes or for wearing my jeans until holes poked through the crotch. None of that mattered. My name was out there. People knew my name. People read my name. Me.

I call it byline fever, but it's more like getting hooked on a drug. The more your byline appears, the more you need it. David Halberstam wrote: "If my byline disappears, have I disappeared as well?"

The byline proved I existed and mattered and had something to say. And it wasn't just any byline, not my name in small humble type, "By Lowell Cohn." It was in letters so big they might have introduced World War III. And my byline didn't include the word *by*. Just my name—a title.

LOWELL COHN

The sheer rush of it all.

And there were benefits. The people I covered knew me, knew the large-lettered LOWELL COHN and had to be respectful of the name and the power of this annoying man. I liked that. Who wouldn't?

My professors at Stanford who thought I was a middle-of-the-road literary scholar—I was—phoned me for all sorts of favors. Would I guest-teach a class in Jane Austen? Like she played second base for the Oakland A's. Would I meet job-seeking undergraduates and preach the benefits of majoring in English? You bet, I would. You study English, you learn to write and think. Would I have lunch with the full professors in English at the faculty club—it would make them so happy? Sign me up.

When I go wine tasting in Sonoma County, the area the *Press Democrat* covers, winemakers come out to greet me with that glazed look on their faces. Someone recently called me "a legend," although this could be the same person who motherfucks me on Twitter.

People want to know, "Are you *the* Lowell Cohn?" I say, "I'm the former Lowell Cohn," now that I'm retired. And, in a way, I feel former. I miss being *the* Lowell Cohn. I'd like a neon sign along Highway 101 between San Francisco and Santa Rosa blinking on and off: LOWELL COHN.

Okay, I'm shallow.

61

GLORY DAYS:
AFTER ATHLETES RETIRE

I NEVER GOT TO KNOW JOE MONTANA, not when he played. After he re-tired, it was another story. It's always another story between athletes and writers after athletes retire—then they become friendly, even close. I'll explain why later on, but first there was one time with Montana the player, a time we connected, if only briefly. And it involved *The Electric Kool-Aid Acid Test* by Tom Wolfe.

This was the mid-1980s and the San Francisco 49ers had won two Super Bowls and were the best organization in football, maybe in all of sports. But they still practiced at an old, weather-beaten, wood-frame facility in Red-wood City, California, where fans could watch practice through the chain-link fence and everyone felt comfortable. The NFL was more innocent then. Maybe the world was. Now the 49ers practice in a guarded compound in Santa Clara.

It was after practice on a weekday and I was in the locker room talking to players who had showered and were going home for dinner and to study the game plan. Tight end John Frank asked me to linger. He was blond and handsome and so young. He already had one Super Bowl ring. During the offseason, he attended Ohio State University College of Medicine. He was a good, tough player and he was reading *The Electric Kool-Aid Acid Test*, Tom Wolfe's nonfiction book about Ken Kesey and his Merry Pranksters who took LSD and traveled around the country in a Day-Glo-colored school bus called *Furthur*. Frank asked if I'd read it. I said yes.

"Please sit down," he said, pointing to a chair at the next locker, which was vacant by now. He took out the book and turned to a page with this famous Kesey quote: "There are going to be times when we can't wait for somebody. Now, you're either on the bus or off the bus. If you're on the bus, and you get left behind, then you'll find it again. If you're off the bus in the first place—then it won't make a damn."

"I keep thinking about that quote," Frank said, his voice earnest. "What does it mean to you?" He was asking my opinion. This almost never happened, not with an athlete.

I was getting ready to answer when Montana and Ronnie Lott, who had heard us, pulled up two chairs.

"Don't stop," Lott said. "We're just listening."

Montana smiled his shy smile—his smile was always shy—and he nodded for us to proceed. And now we had a literary seminar.

Instead of answering, I asked Frank what he thought the quote meant. A frown formed over his brow. This was the key issue for him. "It's something about being committed all the way, committed to whatever you do," he said. "Not half-hearted."

I said that made sense to me: "You're on the bus or you're off. You're one of us or you're not."

"Yes," Frank said, as if I'd solved a mystery.

Montana leaned forward and Lott made a rumbling sound in his throat.

"Do you like the book?" I asked Frank.

"I do," he insisted. "They're having fun. They go wherever they want."

He was reading more these days, he told us: Wolfe and also Kesey. He'd read *One Flew Over the Cuckoo's Nest*.

He asked if I liked Kesey. I said I did. I said *Cuckoo's Nest* explained an entire generation. I said Kesey had studied writing at Stanford, right down the road. Frank said he didn't know that.

He was trying to broaden himself, he said, to think about new things. Montana and Lott listened carefully, studied him. Frank was thinking of getting off the bus, although he probably didn't know it. So obvious in hindsight. In the 1989 Super Bowl he would go on to catch two passes from Montana, one on the winning touchdown drive. He would leave the bus right after that to become a doctor, his NFL career lasting five seasons. But this moment in the old locker room was years before the end. Frank was questioning the meaning of his life in football through the Kesey quote.

"That was very interesting," Lott said when we were done. "I haven't read the book but I will. Thanks for letting me listen."

I looked at Lott and Montana. *Ronnie and Joe are firmly on the bus*, I told myself. *Joe drives the bus.*

I started to leave, but Montana lingered. We were alone now. He wanted to talk—an all-time first. He spoke about going to Notre Dame. Not playing quarterback for Notre Dame. Going to Notre Dame. Something in Frank's tone, in Frank's yearning, had brought Montana back to his young adulthood, to before he became Joe Montana, the institution.

He said there were two student bars in South Bend. One was so crowded patrons had to stand sideways for people to move past. Montana stood sideways to demonstrate extreme crowdedness.

"The other bar was near it," he said. "It was similar to the bar everyone went to, but it was empty and almost no one drank there. It was so strange. Can you tell me why one bar was crowded and one was empty?"

I had no idea, but I struggled to find one. I wanted to encourage him, keep the door open. But he said it didn't matter. Still, he had gone back in time, let down his guard for a moment. Then, just as quickly, he grabbed his clothes and left. We'd never talked personally before, just football stuff at appointed times. His personality was like a mist. That's how I experienced him. I never could grab hold. There was the shy smile, the verbal evasions, the quick exit. But this one time I realized someone was in there, someone I didn't know. I'd been granted a glimpse.

We rarely talked after that. He shut the door, slammed it shut. He was wary of me. I don't blame him. Mostly he avoided me and my colleague from the *San Francisco Chronicle*, Ira Miller. We could be tough, at times too tough. Montana talked to other writers, so he was not media-averse or a snob. Just Lowell- and Ira-averse. I always thought that was fair.

All this changed after he retired. It always changes when players retire. The guard permanently comes down. Enemies become friends. When Montana and I see each other, we talk easily. We are comfortable and look each other in the eye. When he sees Ira, he slides his arm around Ira's shoulder and grins.

A few years ago, a writer from my paper, the *Santa Rosa Press Democrat*, wanted to interview Montana. The sports editor asked if I would contact Montana. I got a message to him. He called back right away. "Lowell, it's Joe."

It's Joe?

I said it was nice to hear his voice. He said it was nice to hear mine.

He asked what I needed. I explained about the interview. He said, sure. I said we couldn't pay him much. He laughed. "Don't worry about that," he said. "I'm happy to do it. I'm doing it for you."

Doing it for me?

*****

Which leads to the truth about athletes and writers—an enduring truth I can demonstrate again and again. Athletes may hate a writer—like me. May think he's out to get them, unfair, a scumbag. After athletes retire, they are freed from the pressure, from the ever-present fear of failure, of being cut, traded, criticized. They become regular people, no longer just athletes. They are like the rest of us. No one makes hotel reservations or plane reservations for them or launders their uniforms or gives them a per diem. Now, they do their own shopping at the grocery store, take out the garbage, share everyday reality with everyday people. They are likable in a normal way. Writers are no longer a threat. Just people. Finally, athletes and writers get along.

But the aging of athletes doesn't explain their new, cordial relationship with writers—doesn't fully explain it. Something else is going on.

History.

Writers like me shared the best time of the athletes' lives. We chronicled their greatness and bore witness in print. When Montana or Lott or Jerry Rice see me, they see themselves back when. I remind them of who they were.

In 2017, I bumped into Lott at a dinner for the Bay Area Sports Hall of Fame. He hugged me a long time. He never hugged me when he played.

When Tony La Russa managed the Oakland A's, he had a TV near the ceiling in front of his office desk. He would talk to me, sure, but often he looked at games on the TV. I was not worth his full attention. Now I see La Russa and we chat, and his manner is warm and his smile radiates.

Harris Barton was an offensive lineman for the 49ers. His teammates liked him. Steve Young liked him. I did, too. But Barton was moody. Sometimes I'd talk to him. He wouldn't answer and then he'd just walk away. Huh?

A few years ago, I went to dinner at Chez Panisse in Berkeley and there was Barton at a table with his wife and some friends. He saw Ira Miller and me, leapt up, dragged us to the table, introduced us. "These are two legendary sports writers," he announced. Proud to know us.

Former welterweight champion Ray Leonard, the best fighter of his era, was involved in a promotion in Northern California. A public-relations person gave him my number so I could write an article about him. Leonard phoned and, before I could ask any questions, said, "It's been a long time, Lowell." Said it with such feeling. I had covered his entire career. I had been there.

The last few years of my career, I appeared weekly on a local TV sports channel, gave commentary in a group discussion. Before the show, I would mingle in the greenroom with people I'd covered: retired athletes—pitcher Shawn Estes, shortstop Rich Aurilia, second baseman Bip Roberts, pitcher Vida Blue, pitcher Bill Laskey, defensive lineman Dennis Brown, and others. In the greenroom and on TV we were equals. They were retired and I was not a writer begging for a quote or being submissive. We shared ideas. We agreed or disagreed. We got along.

I was alone one day in the greenroom with Randy Winn who'd played outfield for the Giants from 2006 to 2009. We had on our makeup and were waiting to go on air. We were alone. I knew Winn from covering him. Not well. He had always struck me as thoughtful and sensitive. Meaning he was aware of his feelings and my feelings and everyone's feelings. A good guy. No attitude. But we never had talked deeply and, although he was polite, I found him guarded. Didn't reveal himself. That day in the greenroom, probably to avoid the awkwardness of silence, I asked if he missed playing. He thought about the question. Thought a long time. I had stumbled upon a vital subject, it seemed. He smiled a sad smile. "No," he said.

I was surprised. Ballplayers miss playing, miss the identity of Big Leaguer—some call retirement the small death. I asked why he didn't miss it.

"I loved playing in the big leagues, don't get me wrong," Winn said. "But I don't miss it. I don't miss being in a batting slump and lying in bed in a road city and wondering why I'm not hitting, going over my at-bats from that night's game again and again, and seeing where I didn't do well. Lying there unable to sleep. I don't miss that. I wouldn't want to do it again."

This was post-retirement talk, greenroom talk. An admission to an ally— not an antagonist. An admission to someone who understood. Winn never would have revealed so much as a player. Dangerous. Teammates reading about his anguish might have considered him soft. A writer could use it against him—that's how a player would think. Now Winn had nothing at stake and he was explaining himself, confessing.

✶✶✶✶✶

Finally, this.

Giants first baseman Will Clark and I were tense around each other at the start of his career. This was the 1980s. We are friendly now. He is a warm, life-embracing man, but at that point we were young and both needed to learn diplomacy. The things I wrote annoyed him. He once gave me the finger, and I probably deserved it.

The Giants were playing a day game at Candlestick Park and, although Candlestick had a bad reputation because of wind and cold, it was beautiful for day games. A filtered sun, warm, light breezes. Perfect for baseball. I arrived at the park early and, instead of heading into the clubhouse, I sat in the dugout. Enjoying myself. No one else there. Peaceful. Until Will Clark walked out of the tunnel from the clubhouse, walked into the dugout. Saw me.

It was then the transformation took place. He was a handsome young man when he felt relaxed. But when he was tense—say, when he was at bat with the bases loaded or when he faced a hostile journalist—his face underwent an extreme change. His jaw moved forward as if it were on tracks. And his eyes became demonic.

This face had a name and the name had a derivation. In Clark's rookie year, San Francisco catcher Bob Brenly was looking through the Giants media guide. He came across Clark's middle name. Nuschler.

"Holy shit," he said. "Nuschler? What's a Nuschler?"

Turns out Nuschler is a family name from a Clark ancestor, an honored name in the Clark family. Brenly didn't know from that. He knew from Nuschler. And he named Clark's fierce competition face the Nuschler Face. And it stuck.

So, I was on the dugout bench enjoying the morning sun, when a happy-go-lucky Clark appeared. He eyeballed me and then he went full Nuschler. That face! God save me! He picked up a bat and paced back and forth in front of me. I could see the headline in my paper: Clark Goes Berserk and Assaults Columnist.

And I could imagine Clark's quote: "Cohn had it coming. All of us feel that way. If it wasn't me, it would have been someone else."

I sat there without moving, didn't want to provoke Clark. He finally stopped in front of me, glaring at me, gripping the bat. *Here it comes*, I thought, ready to die. But he didn't slug me. Instead he said these words I've never forgotten:

"Lowell Cohn, you think you're so fucking smart."

"I don't think I'm so smart, Will."

"Yes you do. I want to tell you this. When I was in college, I read Shakespeare and all that shit."

That right there is the greatest, most interesting quote any athlete ever laid on me.

Shakespeare and all that shit!

Clark walked out of the dugout leaving me alone to contemplate his wisdom. In college, Shakespeare was part of the general shit, a course you had to get through, along with the American Political System, Introduction to Logic, Geology, and Gym. I knew where Clark was coming from. And I was glad to be alive.

We laugh about his quote when we see each other these days, and with a friendly laugh, he says, "Tell me the Shakespeare story, Lowell." Which I happily do.

JIM HARBAUGH
SAYS GOODBYE

T HE ONLY SPORTS PERSON—athlete, coach, owner—who said goodbye to me was Jim Harbaugh. He wrote me a personal letter after I
retired. Not an email. A letter on fine stationery with the University
of Michigan Athletics letterhead. He addressed me as *Mr. Cohn*, although
we had known each other a long time, and he signed it *Respectfully, Jim Harbaugh*, his signature with an upward tilt, a man up for things, enthusiastic,
optimistic.

Harbaugh, who had read a column about my father and me, told me
about his dad, Jack, whom he loves the way I loved my dad. We share that.
Sons who had learned from wonderful fathers. Sons who feel their fathers in
them every day of their lives. I like thinking of Jim Harbaugh as a son—of
a football coach, of course. Harbaugh a man who respects the generations,
who respects tradition and order, everything in its time and place.

He was the least likely person to say goodbye. I got along better with other coaches/managers. Like Bruce Bochy, who would invite me into his office for the hell of it. Same for Tony La Russa who spent endless time with me, although he once called me immature. He pronounced it *im-matoor*. I probably was.

In some ways the relationship between the media and Harbaugh was fraught. He took umbrage—yes, umbrage—at certain questions, would dismiss the reporter with stock phrases: 1) "We've plowed that ground already." 2) "That's low-hanging fruit." 3) "You're asking about scheme. I don't talk about scheme."

He was impatient with reporters who held him accountable but didn't understand football. Who were they to question him? It's like someone who doesn't read books criticizing Saul Bellow for writing about Chicago. But if a writer knew football, actually understood Y-Stick Lookie, a standard offensive play in Harbaugh's book as it was in Bill Walsh's, and if the writer asked Harbaugh about it, a warm smile would spread across Harbaugh's square-jawed, handsome face and he would discuss the play because he was in love with football. It was a matter of the right vocabulary and grammar. You had to show Harbaugh you had both.

In Y-Stick Lookie, the primary receiver often is the tight end, who runs a short pattern up the middle, sticks his foot in the ground, and turns around to face the quarterback. That's the Y-Stick part of the play, a quarterback-friendly route. Although the tight end is the primary receiver, the quarterback has the option to throw the ball to the other receivers, especially the deep "go" route if the cornerback is playing bump-and-run coverage on the flanker and the quarterback likes the matchup. That is the Lookie, the quarterback looking for the receiver far down the field.

Harbaugh refused to accept praise from writers, didn't respect their praise, would say praise made him suspicious. This was not a mere fancy. It was a code he received from Bo Schembechler, his stern, demanding coach at the University of Michigan where Harbaugh played quarterback. "When your team is winning," Schembechler told his players, "be ready to be tough, because winning can make you soft. On the other hand, when your team is losing, stick by them. Keep believing."

Harbaugh has a horror of being soft.

And he lives by another Schembechler quote, a way-of-life statement:

"By your own soul learn to live.
If some men force you, take no heed.
If some men hate you, have no care.
Sing your song, dream your dreams.
Hope your hopes, and pray your prayers."

Harbaugh was independent in the extreme, sometimes annoyingly independent. But he would allow writers to argue with him, would allow me to argue. Bill Belichick regularly cuts off discussion—journalists don't have the right to question him. Harbaugh granted the right, loved the verbal give-and-take. Loved the contest. I would ask a question Belichick might have considered rude or combative, but Harbaugh would smile, a Burt Lancaster grin taking over his face. And he would argue as if we were in a graduate-school seminar on football, each defending his position to the death.

Life for Jim Harbaugh is a contest. It is a key to his personality. Not *the* key—there is no such thing as *the* key in a human being. Merely a key. As the younger brother to Baltimore Ravens coach John, Jim always was competing to be the best even at the most simple things. Wanted to be the tallest, the smartest, the fastest. Everything was a contest. Even eating. Who could drink his milk in one long gulp, who could eat the pork chop fastest? He always was looking for approval. He got it by winning. He measured his life with a scoreboard. Even in press conferences he wanted to win, but he wanted a fair fight.

He and 49ers CEO Jed York ruined their relationship. I imagine mutual destruction. Mutual misunderstanding. When it came to hiring coaches, Harbaugh was York's shining accomplishment. Harbaugh saved York kicking and screaming from his youthful ignorance and inadequacy. In Harbaugh's first season, 2011, he took a 6-10 team to a 13-3 record, took it to the NFC Championship Game. In his four seasons as 49ers head coach, Harbaugh went to three NFC Championship Games and one Super Bowl which he lost to his brother. Harbaugh was a smart tactician but his brilliance lay in leadership. He hoisted the 49ers on his passion, his anger, and his pride, insisted on excellence. And he got it.

He could not understand York—the deference he owed an owner. He was a football coach through and through and anything not directly related to winning—like making nice to the owner—was a waste of time.

Just before the 49ers opened Levi's Stadium in 2014, Harbaugh conducted a team practice in the new stadium. Big to-do. Lots of media. But the grass would not hold. Chunks came up. Players fell. Fiasco. Harbaugh immediately canceled practice and marched his team out of the stadium. A big fuck-you to York, who couldn't even get grass right. Media uproar. There hadn't been so much talk about grass since Walt Whitman.

Bill Walsh would have handled the grass controversy more diplomatically. Anyone would have. Harbaugh came at you straight and he came hard. He projected York and 49ers management as the enemy of the team. This I always felt. Conveyed to the players they were winning for themselves, in spite of the suits who knew zero and got in the way. Nothing unusual about this. Walsh told me he'd be happy if the players hated him, if they played well to spite him. Anything to make the players bond as a team. If Harbaugh made York the common enemy he was following Walsh.

Things came apart when York projected Harbaugh as the enemy. Did it publicly. Thanksgiving night 2014. The 49ers had just lost 19–3 at home to the division-rival Seattle Seahawks. As the forlorn 49ers players and coaches made their way to the losing locker room, York sent out a tweet from his luxury box: "Thank you #49ersfaithful for coming out strong tonight. This performance wasn't acceptable. I apologize for that."

York meant the team didn't come out strong. Harbaugh didn't come out strong. Harbaugh had given York a fuck-you about the grass. And now York was returning the fuck-you. It was a cowardly act, and that's what I wrote. York may not be a coward—I don't know. Maybe he was young and inexperienced. But he and Harbaugh were finished.

Harbaugh coached his final game for the 49ers on December 28, 2014, a 20–17 win over the Arizona Cardinals at Levi's Stadium. When the game ended, he met the media in the auditorium, wouldn't admit he was headed for Ann Arbor. Being the good soldier. When he was done with the media, he walked to his office. He looked around for the final time, pulled off his 49ers sweatshirt and crushed it into a ball. He tossed the sweatshirt into the garbage can near his desk. He headed for the door, walked down a long hallway, walked to the exit, walked into the cool dark star-twinkling night.

63

ELDER ABUSE
ON TWITTER

As I write this I am seventy-three, an old fart who's mentally challenged and doesn't know what month it is. I need to take a nap every day and I should go shit in my hat and I mustn't stop taking my meds and I need to shut up because I'm ancient. All that's for starters. That's every day on Twitter.

Although I'm retired, I still tweet sports because it's a way to keep my toe in the shallow water and I like to express my opinion. As necessary for me as breathing. In a pre-Internet world people disagreed with me by taking the trouble to write a letter. I respected someone who wrote a letter, put it in an envelope and attached a stamp. The letters were almost always polite and, if they were critical, took issue with my point of view. They did not take issue with me—with my right to exist. I always tried to answer the letters.

The Internet changed that. And Twitter is a snake pit. Not that it hurts my feelings. What they write I can take. They want to attack me ad hominem— mostly what Twitter critics do—I wipe my hand across my mouth and move on. But one kind of criticism amazes me, flat-out fascinates me.

It's the go-away-because-you-are-old argument. Not only an attack against me personally—not a rebuttal to my argument—but an attack against all old people. When did it become a crime to grow old?

Twitter twits rarely write homophobic tweets to me, and I don't remember racist tweets or even anti-Semitic tweets, although one critical thinker wrote I should get burned in a German pizza oven. But ageist tweets I receive almost daily.

I have reached a certain age and need to roll away in my wheelchair, play checkers with folks at a nursing home, suck applesauce through a straw, stop dribbling saliva down my chin.

Tweeters—is that the right word?—see nothing wrong with attacking people like me, now in my eighth decade. I assume they are young. I assume they feel empowered by anonymity. I want to write back. Want to ask if they respect their father. Love their grandfather. Want to ask, "Don't you want to grow old?" Want to say, "Your tweet makes you look bad."

But I rarely respond. I mean, what's the point?

64

HELLO GOODBYE:
HOW I DIDN'T SAY
GOODBYE TO STEVE KERR

WHEN THE GOLDEN STATE WARRIORS' 2016–2017 season began, I already knew I would retire in a few months, had informed my paper to rule me out after December 31, 2016. I was in an unusual position, covering things for the final time, already feeling detached, verging on not caring. I always cared.

Early in the season, I covered a Warriors home game, sat in the media interview room for Coach Steve Kerr's pregame session. Kerr is a decent, normal person, a man with a heart. He enjoys verbal give-and-take, but he doesn't project phony intimacy. This I admire about him. He is a pleasure to cover but it never degrades into false friendship or personal expectations on his side or the media's side—at least never on my side. He is a man who knows how to keep his distance behind a smile.

He and I never talked about his life or my life. Our common area was basketball. One time I was on the road with the Warriors in the playoffs following the 2015–2016 regular season, sitting at courtside after a practice with assistant coach Ron Adams who ran the Warriors defense. Adams and I were friendly. We were discussing the prose style of Elmore Leonard, a great American writer, if you'll excuse me, up there with Saul Bellow and Philip Roth. We were saying Leonard never wrote a great novel, no *Augie March* or *American Pastoral*, although *Get Shorty*, *Rum Punch*, *Freaky Deaky*, *City Primeval*, and *Hombre* fall into a specific category: the one-hell-of-a-book-without-being-a-great-book category. But Leonard wrote unbeatable prose, declarative, vivid, and with the best dialogue.

Well, Adams and I were deep into the virtues of Leonard when Kerr walked toward us. I thought he would stop. I thought he would have opinions on Elmore Leonard and I wanted to hear them. I thought he, at least, would acknowledge us. But he didn't. He never looked at us, just kept walking right out of the arena engulfed in his own thoughts, whatever they were. And I thought, *I know you, Steve, but I don't know you at all.*

So, I was there in the media room for his pregame session at an early-season game in 2016, my final season. Some of the reporters wanted to know about the addition of superstar Kevin Durant to the roster—"How will KD coexist with Stephen Curry?" They kept referring to Durant as KD. I remember wanting to vomit. In the past, this KD stuff would not have bothered me, but I was burntout and every little offense reinforced my decision to scram.

What was with this KD business, anyway? Was KD a nickname? I mean, that was the best the basketball world and Durant's teammates could come up with, his initials? KD.

The 49ers once had a great defensive lineman Bryant Young, whom the coaches and players called BY.

BY?

Whatever happened to Slim or Rusty or Moose? Real nicknames. Such a lack of imagination in sports.

It is not a reporter's place to refer to an athlete, someone the reporter covers, by a nickname. Never. Never. Never. KD for a reporter is too familiar. When a reporter asks a coach about Kevin Durant, the reporter must refer to him as Kevin Durant or Durant or even Kevin. In direct address to Durant, the reporter could say Kevin but never KD. Same goes for former 49ers coach Steve Mariucci whom some writers called Mooch. Seriously? If all this proves I am old-style, an old fogey, I happily plead guilty. And remember I was done.

So, some reporters were using the KD form. I didn't find the Durant-Curry topic interesting. Had been done to death. I sat in the front row looking up at Kerr on the stage, Kerr trying his best to answer, a benign expression on his face. And I said to myself, *I'm never coming back to the Warriors. I will never cover another of their games.* This was ironic when you consider they would go on to win the NBA championship that season. I didn't know it then and didn't care. But I knew this: the season would go on months after I packed it in. I was a lame duck, a short-termer.

As I made my decision not to attend, not to care, I felt like the bad kid in high school. You remember that kid. He had checked out long ago, stared out the window, didn't even hear the teacher talking. Flunked English or wood shop or gym and didn't give a damn. I was that kid, and I had never been that kid. I was the good kid always getting high grades (*marks* we called them in New York), and kissing up to the teachers. But, secretly, I always admired the bad kid, and now I was the bad kid and it felt great.

I smiled at Kerr. Sitting high on the dais, he smiled back at me. As I smiled, I thought, *You're on your own, Steve. Have a good rest of your life.*

I never said goodbye to Steve Kerr that night or after I retired, never phoned him or emailed him or dropped by his office. Never did any of that. I walked away from him and Giants manager Bruce Bochy, and Giants head of baseball operations Brian Sabean and Giants CEO Larry Baer and Oakland A's head of baseball operations Billy Beane and Warriors president of basketball operations Bob Myers, men I had known forever, men I liked in a certain way.

I never said goodbye because it seemed unnecessary, entirely beside the point, and because, in a sense, I never said hello.

AFTERWORD

Dear Mr. Cohn,

Heartfelt congratulations to you on the occasion of your retirement from the *Press Democrat*! You are a man I truly respect because of your principles and convictions. Your passion and work ethic are at the highest level, your sense of humor and dry wit were always appreciated, and your mannerisms and facial expressions were pure genius. I couldn't take my eyes off you! They were the highlights of every presser. So much so that I looked forward to seeing you each week even as you were holding us accountable.

Watching you and your son, Grant, do your thing alongside one another and the mutual respect and admiration you show for each other was special for me because of my own relationship with my father. I can tell that your father taught you well. Your stories about describing the triple play to your blind, lawyer father who took you to the Mets-Dodgers game in New York and your prepping him for his cases by reading to him were powerful to me.

I am sure that a savvy veteran like yourself knows how much I respect and like you and Grant. I am not very good at hiding that from those I admire. Still, I didn't want to just tell you that for fear that you might take any heat off your fastball! I enjoyed the challenge.

It was a joy watching you and Grant work alongside each other just as you and your father might have. We share something in common—we are both the products of extraordinary fathers who had uncommon trust in us.

Today, your dad would be so proud of you, just as I know Grant is.

I am and always have been a fan of yours and Grant's!

Respectfully,

Jim Harbaugh
Head Coach, University of Michigan

ACKNOWLEDGMENTS

THANKS TO THE FOLLOWING FOR THEIR GENEROUS CONTRIBUTIONS, counsel and support:

James Barger, Barry Bloom, Vida Blue, Will Clark, Grant Cohn, Carylann Dauber, Marc Flitter, Gary Furness, Ann Killion, Doris Kimmel, Eric Kimmel, Ken Korach, Jerry Kram, Left Coast Mike, Johnnie LeMaster, Kevin Lynch, Bruce MacGowan, Ira Miller, Dave Newhouse, Lisa Olson, Bill Pinella, Carl Steward, Brian Strauss, and Fred vonAppen.

A special thanks to the following for their contributions to my book: Dusty Baker, Jim Harbaugh, Brent Jones, Chris Mullin, Brian Murphy, and Steve Young.

I am deeply grateful to Kirk Reynolds for his help with this project.

A special thanks to Matt Maiocco for introducing my manuscript to Roundtree Press.

Another special thanks to Chris Gruener, the publisher of Roundtree Press, and to Iain R. Morris, Jan Hughes, Mason Harper, and the incredibly talented and patient staff at Roundtree.

And a most special thanks to my wife, Dawn Cohn, the smartest and most generous editor. She transformed this project from a bunch of essays into a book and saved me from embarrassing myself more times than I can count.